Cooking Around the Calendar
with Kids

Holiday and Seasonal Food and Fun

by
Amy Houts

Snaptail Press
Division of Images Unlimited
Maryville, Missouri

All inquiries should be addressed to:
Snaptail Press
Division of Images Unlimited Publishing
P.O. Box 305
Maryville, MO 64468
660-582-4279
imagesun@asde.net   www.snaptail.com

Front cover illustration © Laurie Barrows
Cover design: Kathi Dunn
Interior illustrations: Terri Wilson
Interior layout design: Lee Jackson

ISBN: 0-930643-12-7
Library of Congress Card Number: 2001086052

Houts, Amy
    Cooking Around the Calendar with Kids: Holiday and Seasonal Food and Fun
     Includes index.
    Summary: Cooking with children helps them learn more about food and nutrition
    and the part food plays in all seasons of the year.
       1. Cookery 2. Parenting 3. Children — Nutrition 4. Food — Children 5. Family

First Edition
10 9 8 7 6 5 4 3 2 1

Printed in the United States of America

Contents

Introduction

Cooking is a hands-on activity you can do with children to teach, to create, and to help in their appreciation of the gift of food. Cooking with children is valuable time spent while accomplishing worthwhile tasks.

This book is concerned with the importance of involving children in cooking and preparing food. It is divided into food preparation appropriate for the four seasons. Each season has different foods that taste especially good during that time of year. For example, ice cream is a special treat on a hot summer day, as is hot soup on a cold day. Cooking with a feeling of the changing seasons helps to keep us synchronized with the rhythms of life.

Along with the seasons, there are several factors that affect the food choices we make: the weather, holidays, location, harvest, and family traditions.

Weather - Food choices are greatly affected by the weather. Some people don't enjoy eating when the temperature is hot. Children and adults are often more thirsty than hungry on a hot summer day. You might try serving chilled fruit, vegetables and dip with a variety of cheeses, and a nice, cold fruit drink on those days you don't feel like cooking. During cold winter weather the appetite may increase, perhaps to gain that extra layer of body warmth. A good winter snack choice might be warm apple juice and cinnamon toast.

Holidays - Certain holidays are associated with certain foods. For example, turkey and cranberry sauce go with Thanksgiving. Corned beef and cabbage go together for St. Patrick's Day. These foods become traditional foods for holidays. It's fun to celebrate many holidays from different cultures and to expose children to food from many different ethnic backgrounds.

Location - Where you live determines what is available in the store. Fish and seafood are plentiful on the coast. Beef and pork tend to be popular meat choices in agricultural areas. Foods that are shipped in cost more. We need to be aware of the types of foods produced locally in order to get the best food value for our money. What are the unique foods from your area of the country?

Harvest - In the spring, strawberries and asparagus are plentiful. In the fall, apples and many other fruits and vegetables fill farmers' markets and roadside stands. Even though grocery stores stock many fresh fruits and vegetables all year round, it is best to buy what is in season. The cost will be lower and the quality of the food will be higher, as will the taste.

Family Traditions - Many holiday traditions are associated with food. This differs from family to family because of regional location, ethnic background, religious preference, and/or historical perspective. Perhaps every year your family has an 'end of summer' picnic in the park on the day before school starts. Or maybe certain breads are always baked at holiday time. It is important to share, and fun to create, traditions as a family.

Whatever the reason for your food choices, the time you spend cooking and preparing meals can be more meaningful if shared with children. And what better time is there to set the stage for working with, and enjoying, food than during the early years? Often, too, children are more apt to try new foods if they have a hand in preparing them.

Whether you are a parent, grandparent, teacher, caregiver, or young cook, this book is meant to inspire you to find joy in cooking together. Recipes and food ideas are chosen to give a variety of food experiences appropriate for various age groups. My hope is that this book encourages you to be creative in preparing food with children and that you will cherish your time with each other.

As the seasons change, so too, do food preferences change. May your cooking experiences keep you in harmony with the seasons. And may this book help you find joy in cooking with children all year around.

Happy and healthy cooking!

Amy Houts

Safety in the Kitchen

Safety is the biggest concern when cooking with children. Often we can use common sense to keep our kitchens a safe haven for our children where they can help us cook without being in danger. Yet, with our busy schedules, and the nature of the kitchen environment, we might overlook some safety precautions.

Safety Precautions

Here is a list of suggestions to keep in mind when working in the kitchen:
• Keep sharp knives away from children. Adults should cut foods that are hard enough to require a sharp knife. Children can cut soft foods using a butter knife.
• Don't let children play with small appliances such as mixers, blenders, food processors, can openers, etc.
• Teach children that the range top and oven are hot. Adults should cook foods on the range top and place or remove food from the oven.
• Keep handles on pots and pans turned inward, so there is no danger of someone knocking them off the range.
• Cook hot soup or any hot food on a back burner.
• Keep all cleaners, dish washing detergents, and plastic bags out of your child's reach.
• Do not call vitamins or medicine "candy."

A Word About Choking

Choking can occur when feeding young children. The following foods can cause choking in young children: hot dogs, nuts, seeds, popcorn, raw carrots or celery, whole kernel corn, berries, and small candies. Check with your doctor to determine when to start offering these foods to your child.

Safety Tips

• Cut foods such as hot dogs lengthwise and crosswise (not in circles) before serving.
• Par-boil carrots and celery sticks before serving them.
• Cut foods, such as grapes and cherry tomatoes, in half before serving them.
• Insist your child not talk, walk or run with food in the mouth as this can cause choking with any food.

Teach About Food Safety, Following Directions, and Cooperation

• Teach children about food safety. Foods are easily contaminated by careless handling and needless exposure to germs. The first step to good food handling practices is to work with clean hands. Be a role model by washing your hands with soap and hot water before cooking and requiring children to do the same. As soon as items not related to food are handled, hands need to be washed again. Wear plastic gloves if you have an open sore or cut. Always use a separate spoon when tasting foods. Teach children not to lick the mixing spoon, or fingers, no matter how tempting! To prevent the transfer of bacteria, use separate cutting boards and utensils for raw and cooked meats and vegetables. Promptly refrigerate meats, eggs, and milk. Keep hot foods hot—above 140 degrees F (60 degrees C) and cold foods cold—below 40 degrees F (5 degrees C).

• Teach children to follow directions in the recipe. In all aspects of life, people need to follow certain rules and directions. A recipe is a good place to start. Talk about the recipe. Explain what you will do and what the child will do. Know what needs to be done first, second, and so on. Be sure you have the necessary ingredients and equipment before you begin cooking.

• Emphasize cooperation. Everyone can have a turn or can contribute their part to the recipe or food preparation. Working together cooperatively has many benefits. Children learn to solve problems, to become tolerant of others' ideas, and accept similarities and differences in the way others think and work. Learning to cooperate promotes social behaviors that will help them in their everyday life.

Ten Table Manners Children Can Learn

1. Come to the table with clean hands.
2. Chew with your mouth closed.
3. Wait until everyone is served before you start to eat.
4. Don't talk while chewing.
5. Don't interrupt while others are talking.
6. Ask someone to pass food rather than reaching for it.
7. Don't eat noisily.
8. Don't stuff your mouth.
9. Use your napkin.
10. Ask, "May I please be excused?" when you want to leave the table.

Autumn Ideas

• Make a centerpiece from what can be found on a walk, such as colorful leaves, acorns, etc.

• Make placemats out of fall leaves ironed between pieces of waxed paper.

• Go to a farm stand and let your child choose which vegetables and fruits to buy.

• Check a book out of the library about another culture; cook at least one dish from that culture.

• For Halloween, prepare a meal with your child with all orange food. Some foods you might use: carrots, pumpkin, Cheddar cheese...

• For Thanksgiving, make a list of foods for which you and your child are thankful.

Garden Bounty

As squirrels gather nuts for winter, and ants march together to carry food to their hill, we yearn to be in step with nature to prepare for the long, cold winter ahead. How comforting it is seeing nature's abundance in our very own gardens or farm stands we pass along the road, or even in the produce section of our grocery store boasting "locally grown."

Children can get in the act of gathering, preparing, and cooking while learning some concepts so important to cognitive learning. Children can count the number of tomatoes or other produce you buy. Many foods can be tasted before and after cooking to determine the difference in flavor. Depending on the child's age, ask questions, such as:

> What color is the fruit or vegetable?
> What shape?
> How do they smell?
> Do they have seeds?

Here are some questions to ask about the summer's bounty:

• What is locally grown?
• How can I involve children in preparing this food?
• What would we enjoy the most?
• What is the best price?
• Do I have time to finish the process?
• If the recipe makes a large batch, do I have room in my freezer for the remaining portion?

We can gather fresh fruits and vegetables to enjoy today or to "put up" or freeze to take out at a later date. Then we can once again remember the warm days and refreshing taste of the summer harvest.

Autumn-Rich Tomato Sauce

Tomatoes are enjoyed throughout the summer. Bucketfuls are gathered the day the weatherman predicts the first fall frost. This tomato sauce is perfect when you have several pounds of tomatoes to use; it tastes wonderful and freezes well!

12 pounds tomatoes,
  peeled and diced
3 medium onions, chopped
3 large carrots, sliced
2 green peppers, diced
3 tablespoons oil
2 (6 oz.) cans tomato paste
3 tablespoons brown sugar
1 tablespoon salt
2 teaspoons oregano
1 1/2 teaspoons basil
1/2 teaspoon pepper

Adults must first peel tomatoes by filling a large pot about half full with water. Bring to a boil. Meanwhile, rinse the tomatoes, score with an X on the underside, and remove the core with a paring knife. Then place a few tomatoes at a time in boiling water for about 1 minute, or until the skin begins to peel away from the fruit. Remove tomatoes immediately to a bowl of cool water.

Repeat process until all tomatoes are used. Once cool, children can help peel and discard skin.

Prepare all other vegetables. (A food processor helps, if you have one.)

In a large pot, heat the oil. Sauté the onions, carrots, and peppers over medium heat until light brown, about 10 minutes. Meanwhile, children can help measure out sugar and spices and help cut up the tomatoes. Add to remaining ingredients. Bring to a boil over high heat, then reduce heat to medium-low and simmer, partially covered, for 2 hours. Stir occasionally.

This sauce freezes very well for up to a year. Use 1 pint containers or freezer weight plastic bags. Leave a little room (1-inch) for expansion. Label with contents and date before freezing.

Yield: about 9 pints

Spinach Lasagna

12 lasagna noodles

2 cups (16 oz.) ricotta or *small curd cottage cheese*

1 cup mozzarella cheese

2 tablespoons grated Parmesan cheese

1 egg

1/2 teaspoon dried parsley

1/2 teaspoon salt

1 ½ cups Autumn-Rich Tomato Sauce (p.8) or

1 (16-oz.) jar spaghetti sauce

1 cup cooked spinach (either 1 pound fresh or *10-oz. frozen)*

Cook lasagna noodles in boiling water according to package directions. Drain and cool by placing flat on tin foil. Preheat oven to 350 degrees F.

In a medium-sized bowl, children can help mix together ricotta or cottage cheese, 3/4 cup mozzarella cheese, Parmesan cheese, egg, parsley, and salt. Drain spinach in a strainer; children can help press out excess liquid with a spoon.

In a 9 x 9-inch pan, spoon about 1/4 cup Autumn-Rich Tomato Sauce or spaghetti sauce. Arrange 4 lasagna noodles, slightly overlapping, over sauce. Trim noodles to fit in pan; reserve to make last layer. Spread 1/3 of cheese and egg mixture over noodles, then 1/3 of spinach, and about 1/4 cup sauce. Repeat twice, ending with noodles. Top with remaining sauce and the 1/4 cup mozzarella cheese.

Cover with foil. Bake 35 minutes or until hot and bubbly.

Remove foil and bake 10 more minutes. Let stand 5 minutes before serving. Yield: 4 - 6 servings

Variation for Beef Spinach Lasagna: add 1 pound cooked ground beef to Autumn-Rich Tomato Sauce or spaghetti sauce.

Dried Herbs

Thyme and marjoram are easy to dry. Children can cut sprays from the garden or pick out a bunch from the market. Tie a few branches together and hang upside down in an airy room or loft, or anyplace where it is not damp. In two to three weeks, when brittle to the touch, children can crumble them into airtight containers. What an aroma!

Veggie Pizza

1 package refrigerated crescent rolls
1 (3 oz.) cream cheese, softened
1/2 cup mayonnaise
1/4 cup sour cream
1/2 envelope ranch dressing mix
2 tablespoons milk
4 green onions, cut up
2 carrots, grated
1 tomato, cut in small pieces
1/2 cup cauliflower, sliced thin
1/2 cup broccoli, cut in small pieces

Heat oven to 375 degrees F. Unroll dough and place in ungreased 15 x 10 x 1-inch pan. Children can press dough to form base of pizza. Seal perforations.

Bake for 12 to 15 minutes, or until golden brown. Cool completely.

Children can mix together cream cheese, mayonnaise, sour cream, and ranch dressing mix in a small bowl. Slowly add milk, adding more as needed for a spreading consistency. Blend until smooth. Spread over cooled crust.

Over this sprinkle the cut up vegetables. Refrigerate. To serve, cut into small squares.

Yield: 20 small squares

Sloppy JoAnnes

1 pound ground beef
1 onion, chopped fine
2 stalks celery, chopped fine
1 green pepper, chopped fine
1/4 cup Worcestershire sauce
1/2 cup Autumn-Rich Tomato
   Sauce (p. 8)
1 tablespoon sugar
1 teaspoon vinegar
1/2 teaspoon hot pepper sauce
1 teaspoon salt
1 cup water
4 hamburger buns, toasted

Brown ground beef, onion, celery, and green pepper in a skillet over medium heat. Drain fat.

Children can help measure Worcestershire sauce, tomato sauce, sugar, vinegar, pepper sauce, salt, and water. Add to skillet. Bring to a boil.

Turn down heat, cover, and simmer for 30 minutes. To serve, spoon onto buns.

Yield: 4 hamburger bun servings

Easy Beef Vegetable Soup

1 pound ground beef or
  1 pound ground turkey
1 onion, chopped
3 cups beef broth or water
3 carrots, pared and diced
3 stalks celery, diced
1/4 cabbage, shredded
1 (8-oz.) can tomato sauce
3 tablespoons uncooked rice
1 (16-oz.) can kidney or red beans

Brown ground beef and onion in a 4 qt. pot. Drain fat. Meanwhile, prepare vegetables.

Children can help measure beef broth or water and rice. Add vegetables and meat. Bring to boil, then turn down heat, cover, and simmer for 1 hour.

Easy Variation: Brown 1 pound ground beef. Drain. Add 2 cans condensed vegetable soup and 2 cans water. Heat and serve.

Yield: 6 servings

Garden Salad

For a delicious, refreshing, and crisp lunch-time or anytime treat, try this salad.

1 head Romaine lettuce, torn in
  small pieces
1/2 bunch green onions, chopped
1/2 red pepper, cut in strips
1 small bunch broccoli, cut up
1 package Ramen noodles
1 cup English walnuts, chopped
2 tablespoons butter

Dressing:
1/2 cup oil
1/3 cup sugar
1/4 cup wine vinegar
2 tablespoons soy sauce

Prepare lettuce, onions, pepper, and broccoli. Children can mix all vegetables in a bowl. Place in refrigerator.

Children can slightly crush Ramen noodles by placing them in a plastic bag and lightly rolling over them with a rolling pin. Sauté English walnuts in butter. Add noodles. Set aside.

In jar, place dressing ingredients and shake well to dissolve.

Drizzle dressing over lettuce and vegetable mixture just before serving. Gently mix. Then add walnut-noodle mix. Serve.

Yield: 4 - 6 servngs

Apple-Cabbage Salad

A simple but tasty salad—children enjoy this non-traditional coleslaw.

2 cups shredded cabbage
1 cup shredded carrots
1 cup diced, unpeeled apple
1 teaspoon celery seed
2 tablespoons olive oil
1 tablespoon fresh lemon juice

Shred cabbage and carrots in a large bowl either with a food processor or a hand shredder.

Children can dice unpeeled apple. Combine all ingredients; mix well.

Refrigerate at least an hour and serve.

Yield: 6 - 8 servings

Microwave Oven Stuffed Peppers

6 medium green peppers
1 1/2 pounds lean ground beef
1 cup cooked brown rice
1 small onion, chopped
Salt and pepper to taste
1 cup Autumn-Rich Tomato Sauce

Cut off top of green pepper. As you remove the seeds and membrane, discuss how the pepper grows on a vine.

In a medium sized bowl, children can mix together the (uncooked) beef, rice, onion, salt, and pepper. Spoon the meat mixture into each pepper and place in a casserole dish.

Peppers should touch in baking dish so steam and heat conduction help them cook. Pour Autumn-Rich Tomato Sauce over peppers.

Cover with lid and cook 30 minutes on high power (625 watts). If using temperature probe, set at 175 degrees F.

Let peppers stand covered 5 minutes before serving.

Serves 4 - 6

Microwave Oven Rules to Follow

Always have adult supervision.
Always use microwave safe dishes (no metal).
Always close door securely.
Always observe safe procedures.

Children can help with:
• measuring, pouring, mixing, and preparing
• opening and closing the microwave oven door
• pushing the buttons for the microwave controls

Microwave ovens are best used for:
• keeping the kitchen cool
• warming breads and rolls
• heating/re-heating
• defrosting frozen foods
• making quick snacks
• cooking vegetables
• preparing foods quickly
• melting foods such as
butter and margarine, cheese, and chocolate

Conventional ovens and range tops are best used for:
• browning foods
• crispy foods
• sauces and gravies
• baked goods

Carrot-Honey Muffins

1 cup unbleached flour
1/2 cup whole wheat flour
2 1/2 teaspoons baking powder
1/2 teaspoon baking soda
1/2 teaspoon salt
1/2 teaspoon cinnamon
1/8 teaspoon allspice
1 cup carrots, coarsely grated
1/4 cup chopped nuts
1/2 cup raisins
1 egg
1/2 cup milk
1/4 cup vegetable oil
1/4 cup honey

Children can stir together flours, baking powder and soda, salt, and spices in large bowl. Add grated carrots, nuts, and raisins to mixture.

In small bowl, beat egg; add milk, vegetable oil, and honey. Pour over flour mixture. Stir just until dry ingredients are moistened.

Children can grease twelve muffin cups, or place paper baking cups in pans. Fill muffin cups 3/4 full. Bake in 375 degrees F oven for 20 minutes. Serve warm.

Yield: 12 muffins

Zucchini Squares

1 cup brown sugar
1/4 cup sugar
3/4 cup butter
2 eggs
1 1/2 teaspoons vanilla
1 3/4 cup flour
2 teaspoons baking powder
2 cups shredded raw zucchini,
  drained
1 cup coconut
1 cup chopped walnuts

Cream sugars and butter. Add eggs, one at a time. Add vanilla. Stir in flour and baking powder.

Children can stir in zucchini, coconut, and walnuts.

Spread batter evenly in a greased 13 x 9-inch pan.

Bake at 350 degrees F for 35 - 40 minutes.

Yield: 24 squares

Back-to-School

Breakfast Ideas

The word breakfast comes from the phrase "break the fast." Your body has been fasting for about 12 hours, from the time you ate supper or a bedtime snack the night before. At breakfast your child begins to take in some of those nutritious foods he needs for growing.

In order for your child to feel his best when he's learning important concepts, offer him a healthy breakfast. Although the traditional breakfast of eggs and bacon is high in protein, it is also high in fat and cholesterol. This hearty breakfast can be reserved for a once-in-a-while treat. Doughnuts, coffee cakes, and other high-fat or high-sugar foods should also be limited.

Most breakfast protein should be centered on items from the grain group, such as low-sugar cereals and whole-grain breads that contain fiber. Fiber is found only in plant foods such as whole grains, fruits, and vegetables.

There are two types of fiber: insoluble and soluble. Children and adults need both types in their diet. Insoluble fiber, sometimes called "bulk," is good for digestion and is found in whole grains. Soluable fiber is found in beans and oats. This type of fiber may help lessen the risk of heart disease. Breakfast foods are perfect ways to get the amount of fiber your body needs for good health.

Here are suggestions to get you and your child off to a good start:
• For whole grain cereals, try mixing 2 or more cereals in bowls for a contrast of textures and flavors.
• Use granola to sprinkle over store bought whole grain cereal for that extra sweetness and crunch.
• Sprinkle hot oatmeal with fresh apple bits and cinnamon.
• Try different kinds of bagels: whole wheat, pumpernickel, blueberry, etc. Toast and spread with light cream cheese, or butter or margarine topped with Swiss or Cheddar cheese.
• For a taste-change in muffins, try whole grain, bran, or fruited.
• Top English muffins with apple slices and cheese.
• Spread whole wheat biscuits with low or no sugar jams.
• Spread whole wheat bread with sugar and cinnamon.
• Toast whole grain bread, spread with peanut butter, and top with banana slices.
• Toast raisin bread and spread with butter or margarine.
• Top whole grain pancakes or waffles with fruit and yogurt.
• Make French toast with whole grain bread; top with cottage cheese and maple syrup.
• Serve banana slices with cottage cheese; sprinkle with wheat germ.
• Make fruit salads, preferably with fresh fruit. If canned fruit is used, buy the type packed in fruit juices.
• Prepare any flavor breakfast milk shake and serve in a special glass.

Unforgettable Granola Cereal

4 cups old-fashioned
  or quick cooking rolled oats
 1 cup honey
1 cup vegetable oil
1 cup cold water
1 cup soy flour
1 cup wheat germ
1 cup hulled sunflower seeds
1 cup chopped walnuts or pecans
1 cup flaked coconut

Preheat oven to 300 degrees F. Children can measure and mix oats, honey, and oil together in a large bowl. Add all remaining ingredients and mix well. Spread mixture evenly on a large, greased cookie sheet. Bake 1 hour.

After cooling, crumble, and store in an airtight container in the refrigerator. Serve with milk.

Yield: about 10 cups

Note: honey, nuts, and seeds are not recommended for young children. Brown sugar can be substituted for honey, and extra oats for nuts and seeds.

Three Grain Refrigerator Muffins

These muffins are a treat for breakfast. Bake a batch of these for those busy days ahead.

2 cups bran cereal
2 cups quick cooking rolled oats
2 cups wheat cereal
2 cups boiling water
1 cup butter or margarine
2 1/2 cups sugar
4 eggs, beaten
5 cups flour
5 teaspoons baking soda
1 tablespoon salt
1 quart buttermilk

Pour water over cereals; let cool. Children can cream butter or margarine and sugar in a large bowl. Add eggs and cereal mixture. Mix until blended. Add dry ingredients alternately with the buttermilk until all are mixed in. Batter will be stiff. Use immediately or place in a tightly covered bowl and keep refrigerated.

To bake, preheat oven to 400 degrees F. Children can spoon batter into greased or paper-lined muffin cups. Bake for 20 minutes.

Remove from muffin tin and cool on wire rack.

Yield: about 5 dozen muffins

Note: This batter will keep 30 days in a covered container in the refrigerator.

Planning Lunch

When my daughter Emily turned 5 she was able to stay for the extended preschool program, which lasted until 1 pm. How excited she was to be able to eat lunch with her friends and her teacher!

 The following suggestions provide tips on planning and preparing lunch. It can be made nutritious and appealing with very little effort. Following the Food Guide Pyramid provides a basic format for good nutrition.

The Food Guide Pyramid
for children 2 to 6 years indicates:
6 servings from the grain group
3 servings from the vegetable group
2 servings from the fruit group
2 servings from the milk group
2 servings from the meat group
limit calories from fats and sweets

For older children and adults the
guidelines indicate:
6-11 servings from the grain group
3-5 servings from the vegetable group
2-4 servings from the fruit group
2-3 servings from the milk group
2-3 servings from the meat group
use fats and oils sparingly

Variety of Foods

Lunch is more than a snack. A snack should include a drink and one to two items from the food pyramid, such as milk, crackers, and apple slices. Lunch might be called an "extended snack."

Breads, grains, fruits, and vegetables should make up the largest portion of the lunch. Beans, poultry, fish, eggs, and nuts as well as milk, yogurt, and cheeses can complete the meal. Even if children don't eat foods from each section of the pyramid for every meal, they can eat these foods within each day, or every few days. You may not be there to see what they chose to eat from the lunch you packed, but you can offer a variety of nutritious foods.

Making Foods Fun

There are several quick and easy ways to make lunches more fun. Cut a sandwich into your child's initial. Use a variety of animal cookie cutters to cut sandwich shapes. Add crunch and texture by including fruit and/or vegetable bits to sandwiches or salads.

My child loves having a picture-note stuck in with her lunch. She recognizes her name written on a slip of paper, or a simple message such as, "I ♥ you". I add upbeat symbols: flowers, rainbows, etc. by hand or with a sticker.

Get Organized

The night before is a good time to make lunch and leave it in the refrigerator overnight. Mornings can be very hectic. Sunday evening may be an appropriate time to make items you will be freezing for the week ahead.

A good time-saving and management tip is to plan meals for the entire week. Your child can provide input into the planning. Look through published school lunch menus and decide when he or she wants to eat at school, if appropriate, or to bring a lunch. Post your menu in a prominent place like the refrigerator, for quick reference.

Children can help with lunch according to their age and ability.

Children can help by:
• deciding what to have (with your guidance)
• mixing salad
• placing foods in reusable plastic container or wrapping food in plastic wrap
• placing food in lunch box or sack
• wiping counters after lunch is prepared
• spreading peanut butter on bread
• making lunch all by themself

Just as soon as your child wants to help, let her learn this skill in taking care of herself. In the coming years, your child should grow into taking responsibility for her lunch.

Cereal Mix

Here is an easy snack idea that children love to make and eat. This recipe makes a large quantity that will be good for several after-school-time snacks. The variety of shapes make this cereal mix interesting to see, fun to eat, and more delicious!

2 cups circle-shaped cereal
2 cups square-shaped cereal
2 cups sphere-shaped cereal
2 cups small pretzels
2 cups animal crackers

Children can measure and mix all ingredients together in a large bowl. Store in plastic bag. Serve in small (3 oz.) plastic or paper cups. Let children eat this as finger food.

Yield: about 20 servings

Lunch Box Ideas

Although sandwiches are traditional for lunch, there are many possibilities. Refreshing salads made from vegetables, pasta, beans, or rice can be carried in a washable plastic bowl with a lid. (Be sure to include a spoon or fork.) Tempt your child with fruited muffins, crunchy breadsticks, or pretzels. Following are some suggestions and recipes for lunch box treats.

• When planning and preparing lunch, work as a team with your child.

• Depending on your child's likes and dislikes, be creative. Use a bagel, pumpernickel, or pita bread.

• Use a variety of cheeses, such as American, Swiss, Cheddar. Add lettuce, watercress, or other greens.

• Think past the traditional sandwich. Serve pasta salad, fruit and cheese, or veggie sticks and peanut butter.

• Include a variety of foods from the food pyramid: breads and cereal, fruits, vegetables, meats, and milk.

• Extend the nutritional value of the meal, if possible. For example, if your child likes yogurt, (which is similar in nutritional value to a glass of milk) add fruit to the yogurt, or pack granola to be mixed in the yogurt.

• Pack food in small servings. A half sandwich is better than an overwhelming whole one. A few apple slices (dipped in lemon juice so they don't turn brown) packed instead of a whole apple, etc. do not seem overwhelming. To a child, several different food items are better, but don't pack too much. There isn't always time to eat and talk and finish what you have packed during the allotted lunch "hour" (usually 20 - 30 minutes).

Keep it Cool

Unless the lunch will stay refrigerated, you will need to keep food from spoiling. There are several ways to accomplish this:

• freeze bread for sandwiches. It will defrost by lunch time.
• freeze filling for sandwiches (do not freeze mayonnaise).
• freeze juice; place in lunch box. It should defrost by lunch time.
• place a freezer pack or ice pack in lunch box.

19

Go-Togethers

Keep in mind that your child has his or her own personal taste. Here are some ideas for terrific lunch-time combinations. Check off the ones you and your child would like to try.

- [ ] turkey, Swiss cheese, rye crackers
- [ ] ham, American cheese, sesame crackers
- [ ] beef, Cheddar cheese, wheat crackers
- [ ] chicken, Monterey-jack cheese, tortilla chips
- [ ] strawberries/banana, cottage cheese, melba toast
- [ ] tuna fish, gouda cheese, saltine crackers
- [ ] carrot sticks, Muenster cheese, animal crackers
- [ ] peaches, cream cheese, graham crackers
- [ ] tossed green salad, parmesan cheese, bread sticks
- [ ] apple slices, peanut butter, rice cakes

Ants on a Log

Kids love celery stuffed with cheese spread, too!

celery
peanut butter
raisins

Rinse and dry celery branches. Fill hollowed part of celery with peanut butter. Top with raisins.

Cut "logs" into fourths, crosswise.

Banana "Dog"

1 tablespoon peanut butter
1 teaspoon jelly or fruit
* spread (any flavor)*
1 hot dog bun
1 banana
1 teaspoon lemon juice

Children can spread peanut butter and jelly or fruit spread on a hot dog bun. Peel banana. Brush with lemon juice. Put in bun. Wrap or put in sandwich container. Place in lunch box.

Yield: 1 sandwich

Note: An unpeeled banana can be transported in lunch box, then peeled and placed in bun later. (Lemon juice will not be needed.)

Pasta Salad with Variations

1 (8-oz.) package curly noodles,
* cooked, drained*
1 cup diced celery
1/2 green pepper, diced
2 tablespoons Parmesan cheese
1/2 cup Italian (oil and vinegar)
* dressing or mayonnaise*

Children can help mix all ingredients together. Spoon a portion into a small container with a lid, such as a butter or margarine tub. Be sure to include a fork in the lunch box.

Variations:
Add a can of tuna for a main dish salad.
Add 1 sliced, steamed zucchini and 1/4 cup sliced black olives, and cubes of mozzarella cheese.

Yield: 6 - 8 servings

Cherry Tomatoes with Dip

Cherry tomatoes
1/2 cup sour cream or
* plain yogurt*
1/2 cup mayonnaise
1 teaspoon dried minced onion
1/2 teaspoon garlic powder
1 teaspoon celery seed
1 teaspoon seasoning salt

Children can combine all ingredients except tomatoes in a mixing bowl. Mix until smooth. Cover bowl with plastic wrap or foil and refrigerate for several hours or overnight before serving. Wash tomatoes, remove stems, and cut in half.

When ready to eat, stick a toothpick into the cherry tomato halves and dip.

You can also use carrot and celery sticks, cauliflower or broccoli, or other veggies with this dip.

Yield: 1 cup

Chunky Fruit Salad

1 apple, cut into chunks
1 small can pineapple chunks
1 small can mandarin oranges
Few grapes, halved

Wash apple and cut up. Drain pineapple, reserving juice. Drain juice from mandarin oranges and discard. Wash grapes and halve.

Children can combine all fruits, then pour some of the reserved pineapple juice over them. Fill a non-spillable container with this refreshing combination of fruits for packing in child's lunch.

Add other foods you have on hand, such as dates or nuts, or miniature marshmallows for a special surprise.

Yield: 2 cups

Chewy Oatmeal Bars

1/3 cup butter or margarine,
* melted*
1 cup brown sugar
1 egg
1 teaspoon vanilla
3/4 cup all-purpose flour
3/4 cup oatmeal
1/2 teaspoon baking powder
1/2 teaspoon salt

Preheat oven to 350 degrees F. Children can grease a 9 x 9-inch square pan.

Children can mix the melted butter or margarine, brown sugar, egg, and vanilla. Then add the rest of the ingredients, stirring just until mixed. Pour into pan, spreading to corners. Dough will be thick.

Bake for 25 to 30 minutes. Cool. Cut into 20 squares.

Variation for Chocolate Chip Squares: sprinkle 1/2 cup semi-sweet chocolate chips on top of dough before baking.

Yield: 20 bars

Back-to-School Snacks

Emily was sitting next to a friend at snack time. "What is this?" Emily asked as she looked at the rice cake topped with peanut butter.
"It's good!" replied her friend. "Try it."
Emily took a tiny bite. "It is good," she said, and took a bigger bite.

Friends encourage each other to try new foods. Here are snacks foods to try.

Nutritious Snack Foods

Sliced fruits: apples, oranges, bananas, grapes, raisins
Vegetables: carrot sticks, celery sticks with peanut butter, cauliflower or broccoli with dip
Crackers: wheat, rye, graham, cheese, rice, etc.
Crackers topped with: vegetable slices, cheese slices, peanut butter
Sandwiches (1/4 to 1/2 is a snack serving)
Breadsticks, rice cakes, pretzels
Pudding, pudding pops, frozen juice pops
Gelatin with fruit
Plain cookies or cereal bars: vanilla wafers, animal crackers, granola bars

The best snacks are:
· low in salt, sugar, and fat
· low in preservatives
· close to their natural state (not highly processed)

Popcorn

Popcorn is a favorite snack. It tastes good, it's filling, high in fiber, and it can be low-calorie if popped with an air popper and eaten plain. One cup has 25 calories.

Toppings for popcorn
• seasoned salt
• melted butter
• grated cheese, Cheddar, Swiss, or Parmesan
• cinnamon-sugar, and enough melted butter to make it stick

Note: To prevent choking, children under 4 should not eat popcorn.

English Muffin Pizzas

1 English muffin
2 tablespoons tomato sauce
2 tablespoons grated mozzarella
cheese
1 teaspoon Parmesan cheese

Split muffin in half. Toast. Children can spread tomato sauce on each half. Top with mozzarella cheese and Parmesan cheese. Broil for about 1 minute, or until cheese melts and is lightly browned.

Yield: 2 mini pizzas

Cinnamon-Raisin Bread

3 cups buttermilk baking mix
1/2 cup raisins
3 tablespoons sugar
1 teaspoon cinnamon
3/4 cup milk
1 egg, lightly beaten

Preheat oven to 350 degrees F. Grease and flour an 8-inch round cake pan.

In a large bowl, combine baking mix, raisins, sugar, and cinnamon.

Children can stir in milk and egg, just until blended. Pour into prepared pan.

Bake 30 - 35 minutes until golden brown. Cool in pan for 10 minutes. Remove from pan. Cut into wedges. Serve warm with butter.

Yield: 6 servings

Banana Pudding

1 (1 oz.) package instant vanilla
pudding
2 cups milk
2 bananas

Children can stir or shake pudding mix and milk, according to package directions. Peel and slice bananas. Place in serving bowls. Top with pudding. Chill.

Yield: 4 (one-half cup) servings

Variation for Banana Pudding Pie: Reduce amount of milk to 1 1/2 cups. Place banana slices in a graham cracker crust, and pour pudding on top. Chill until firm, about 1 hour. Top with whipped cream.

Apples!

Apple sauce or apple pie, please,
Apple crisp or apple cookies,
Apple dumplings, apple cider,
Apple salad for our supper.

Amy Houts

The versatile apple! Think of all the textures and flavors and contrasts. A fresh apple: sweet and spicy. Apple pie: sweet and yet refreshing. Apple cider: tart, yet refreshing.

Healthful Benefits

Besides its pleasing taste, the apple has many healthful benefits. Perhaps that is why people say, "An apple a day keeps the doctor away."

• High in fiber — the average-sized apple has as much fiber as a bowl of most breakfast cereals.
• Cholesterol free — apples fight cholesterol because the pectin in apples helps with digestion.
• Low in sodium — less sodium than celery, carrots, or even drinking water.
• Rich in vitamins and minerals — fresh apples especially contribute vitamins and minerals to our daily diet.
• Help to keep teeth clean — "nature's toothbrush" is a good after-lunch treat.

Apple Tips

• To keep fresh apples from turning brown when sliced, rub with lemon juice, or place cut apples into a bowl containing a mixture of water and lemon juice.
• Add diced apple to your favorite cabbage slaw or salad for a pleasing change.
• Add diced or grated apple to a muffin recipe or mix.

Apple Activities

• When eating a fresh apple, cut it across, horizontally, and show your child the star in the center of the apple. What a surprise!
• Cut a fresh apple into wedges and position the wedges on a plate in a circle in the shape of a flower, with the wedges as petals.
• Count how many seeds are in your apple.
• Read the tale of Johnny Appleseed.

A Trip to an Apple Orchard

Have you ever visited an apple orchard? It is thick with blossoms and bumblebees in the spring and heavy with apples in the fall.

It is well worth taking your child to an orchard, or going along on a field trip. Here apples are harvested and sorted, packaged and shipped, and might be ground into juice or brewed into cider, candied, frozen or dried, or baked into breads or strudel.

My daughter's class visited a most amazing orchard in Nebraska City called Morton Orchard at Arbor Day Farm, which is owned by the National Arbor Day Foundation. This is a non-profit educational organization dedicated to promoting tree planting and conservation throughout the United States. We visited the Orchard/Apple House and learned about the many varieties of apples grown in the Preservation Orchard—one as big as a grapefruit, and one as small as a plum. Parents enjoyed this trip just as much as the children.

When school starts, so does the time of year for serious apple eaters and apple givers. That might be why the apple is a symbol for teachers. What a simple, yet perfect gift for a teacher—something of the earth, healthy, non-fattening, in beautiful hues of red or green or gold. And if you are asked for suggestions of where to go on a field trip, suggest a trip to an apple orchard!

Included are three apple recipes to try with your child adapted from Lee Jackson's book, *Apples, Apples, Everywhere*, which profiles apple orchards nationwide and their favorite recipes. The cookbook includes over 150 ways to prepare apples. For more apple recipes, check her website at: *www.imagesunlimitedpub.com.*

ABC Muffins
(Apple-Buckwheat-Cinnamon)

1 cup unbleached white flour
1 cup buckwheat flour
2 teaspoons baking powder
2 teaspoons cinnamon
1/2 cup honey
1 egg
1 cup cider (or milk)
1 cup finely chopped apple

Children can help measure and mix together dry ingredients. Add honey, egg, and cider or milk.

Mix only until dry ingredients are moistened. Gently fold in apples. Spoon into well-greased muffin pans.

Bake at 350 degrees F for 15 - 20 minutes.

Yield: 1 dozen muffins.

Leona Heitsch, The Ridge Orchards, Bourbon, Missouri

Double Apple Salad

1 cup boiling water
1 (3 oz.) package orange gelatin
1 cup apple cider
1 cup chopped apple
1/4 cup diced celery
1/4 cup chopped walnuts
Dash of salt (to 1/4 teaspoon)

Pour boiling water over orange gelatin and salt; stir to dissolve.

Add cider; chill until partially set. Children can stir in chopped apple, celery, and walnuts. Spoon into 3-cup ring mold.

Chill until set. Unmold onto lettuce-lined plate.

Yield: 4 (one-half cup) servings

Gayle Irons, Irons' Fruit Farm, Lebanon, Ohio

Apple Cranberry Crisp

3 cups sliced apples
1 (8-oz.) can jellied cranberry sauce
1/2 teaspoon grated orange rind
1 cup oatmeal
1/2 cup flour
1/2 cup brown sugar
1/2 teaspoon cinnamon
Pinch salt
1/3 cup butter or margarine

Children can mix apples, cranberry sauce, and orange rind in greased 8 x 8-inch pan.

Combine remaining ingredients in bowl of food processor and turn on and off until crumbly. Pour crumb topping over apple mixture.

Bake at 350 degrees F for 45 minutes or until browned.

Serve with ice cream, if desired.

Yield: 8 servings

Ann Steele, Stark Brothers Nurseries and Orchards Company, Louisiana, Missouri

Applesauce

6 cooking apples
1/2 cup water
1/4 cup sugar

Adult can pare apples, or depending on age of child, show child how to pare, making the peelings as thin as possible. Adult will need to core apples. Children can cut apples into chunks with dinner knife.

In saucepan, add water to apples. Cover and cook over low heat until apples are soft. Stir occasionally. *Watch carefully so apples do not scorch!*

Break up apples with fork, potato masher, or a blender.

Stir in the 1/4 cup sugar and continue cooking until thickened.

Yield: approximately 4 cups

Apple Fruit Roll

Make applesauce using above recipe.

Preheat oven to 150 degrees F.

Children can cover a 15 x 10 x 1-inch baking sheet with plastic wrap. (Since the oven is at a low temperature, the plastic wrap will not melt.) Spread hot or cold applesauce evenly over the baking sheet so that fruit is no more than 1/4-inch thick.

Dry mixture in oven for 6 - 8 hours. Prop door of oven open slightly to allow the moisture to escape.

After 6 - 8 hours, the mixture should be rubbery and slightly sticky. Children can peel the slab from the pan, roll up, and cut into slices or keep flat and cut into bars.

For variety, add well chopped nuts to the applesauce before drying.

Yield: about 15 slices

Halloween Pumpkins

I have a special feeling each autumn. The air turns cool and I am reminded of a starched cotton dress for that first day of school. In this season colors and flavors haunt me in a comforting way. Shades of orange and brown dot our doorway with the ritual of hanging Indian corn.

Orange is the color of the humble vegetable that grows in autumn—the pumpkin. This "winter squash" is a versatile food. It can be used in pies, puddings, and breads, muffins, cookies, and soups, or eaten like potatoes, mashed with butter. The pumpkin, when carved into a jack o' lantern, is a symbol of Halloween, which is celebrated October 31, the eve of All Saints Day.

Children enjoy picking out symbols of the season to display on a table or buffet. Natural decorations, such as pinecones, apples, buckeyes, acorns, gourds, colored leaves, dried wild flowers, or Indian corn centered on miniature or larger pumpkins, evoke a feeling of the season. Some dried weeds are beautiful. You might want to start a tradition of collecting autumn treasures.

Pumpkin Preparations

The month for pumpkins is October. When your child helps you choose a pumpkin, look for one with a bright orange color that is firm to the touch. Do not choose one that is soft to the touch or has blemishes. If your child wants a large one, you might suggest that you will buy any pumpkin <u>he</u> or <u>she</u> can carry. Also, you might want to buy two, one to make a jack o' lantern and one to cook. (The smaller ones are better for cooking–large pumpkins have stringy pulp.)

Store in a cool, dry place, such as outside in the crisp autumn air, if the temperature is above 32 degrees F. If planning to cook your pumpkin, do so within a month.

A Safe Jack O' Lantern

Instead of cutting facial features for your jack o' lantern, why not plan an alternative activity in which children can take part? They can color the pumpkin with crayons or markers. (Indelible markers stay on best, so closely supervise to see that the pumpkin is the only thing that gets marked.)

Children can use stickers on the pumpkin. Look for eyes, nose, and mouth stickers for more of a traditional jack o' lantern look. Or, you can make your own triangle eyes and jagged mouth out of black construction paper and glue them on.

Pumpkin Teaching Ideas

- go to the pumpkin patch and see how they grow and talk about the size, shape, color, and texture
- count the seeds
- draw pictures of pumpkins with different emotions: happy, sad, angry, and scared jack o' lanterns; talk about feelings.

Cooking Pumpkin

There are three ways to cook pumpkin: baking, boiling, or microwaving. After cooking, pumpkin can be used in recipes or frozen for later use. First wash pumpkin. Then cut in half with a large knife. Your child can help remove the slimy strings and seeds using either his hands or a spoon. Save the seeds, if your wish, to bake. (See page 32.) After cooking, put pumpkin through a strainer for a fine consistency. Use in pies, breads and cookies.

Baked
Place the pumpkin, shell-side up, in a 9 x 9 inch pan or on a cookiesheet. Bake at 325 degrees F. for about 1 hour, or until very tender. (Test with a fork.) Scrape the pulp from the shell and mash.

Boiled
Remove skin from pumpkin with a paring knife and cut into cubes. Heat 1-inch of water to boiling in a large saucepan. Place pumpkin cubes in pot and bring to a second boil. Then turn heat to low, cover, and simmer about 30 minutes.

Microwave
Place the pumpkin, shell side down, in a 9 x 9-inch microwaveable pan. Cover with wax paper. Microwave 15 minutes, depending on size, or until tender. (Test with a fork.) Scrape the pulp from the shell and mash.

Pumpkin Bread

3 cups sugar
1 cup oil
4 eggs
2 cups (16 oz. can) pumpkin
1/3 cup water
3 1/3 cups flour
1/2 cup wheat germ
1 teaspoon baking powder
2 teaspoons baking soda
1 1/2 teaspoons salt
1 teaspoon cinnamon
1 teaspoon nutmeg
1/2 teaspoon cloves

Grease and flour two 9 x 5-inch loaf pans. Preheat oven to 350 degrees F.

In a large bowl, children can stir together sugar and oil. Add eggs, pumpkin, and water.

Add remaining ingredients and stir until combined.

Pour into prepared pans; bake 60 - 70 minutes, or until a toothpick comes out clean.

Yield: 2 loaves

Pumpkin Bars

2 cups sugar
1 cup vegetable oil
4 eggs
2 cups (16-oz. can) pumpkin
2 cups flour
2 teaspoons cinnamon
1/2 teaspoon salt
1/2 teaspoon baking soda
2 teaspoons baking powder
1 cup chopped nuts

Preheat oven to 350 degrees F. Grease a 10 x 15-inch cookie sheet.

Use a large bowl and wooden spoon. Children can beat together sugar, oil, and eggs. Add pumpkin. Stir in flour, cinnamon, salt, baking soda, and baking powder. Add nuts and pour into prepared pan.

Bake for 25 minutes, or until toothpick comes out clean. Cool. Frost with cream cheese frosting.

Yield: 35 two-inch bars

Cream Cheese Frosting
3-oz. cream cheese, softened
6 tablespoons butter, softened
1 teaspoon vanilla extract
Pinch salt
1 3/4 cups confectioners' sugar

Children can beat cream cheese and butter in a medium-sized bowl until blended. Stir in vanilla, salt, and confectioners' sugar.

Frost pumpkin bars.

Toasted Pumpkin Seeds

Wash seeds, discarding strings and orange residue. Separate seeds. Soak overnight in bowl of water to cover seeds and add about 2 tablespoons salt. Then drain water and spread seeds one layer deep on buttered cookie sheet. Bake in 325 degrees F. oven for about 15 minutes or until lightly browned. Stir occasionally while baking. Taste when cool. Sprinkle with salt, garlic salt, or onion salt, if desired.

Here are other variations:

For spicy seeds, mix 2 cups of pumpkin seeds with 1/2 teaspoon Worcestershire sauce, 1 tablespoon vegetable oil, and 1 teaspoon salt. Place on cookie sheet and roast for 1 hour at 250 degrees F. Stir occasionally for even browning.

For "ranch" flavor, mix two cups of pumpkin seeds with 2 tablespoons of vegetable oil. Add a small packet of dry ranch-flavored dressing mix. Stir to coat the seeds. Place on cookie sheet and roast for 1 hour at 250 degrees F. Stir several times to have seeds evenly browned.

To microwave pumpkin seeds, arrange seeds on a glass pie plate. Sprinkle lightly with salt, if desired. Microwave on high for 5 - 7 minutes, or until seeds are crisp. Stir after each minute. Cool.

Store pumpkin seeds in an air-tight container. Place in freezer for long term storage.

*Note: seeds should not be eaten by young children, as choking is possibl*e. See "Safety in the Kitchen," page 3.

Thanksgiving Foods

Come, ye thankful people come,
Raise the song of harvest-home,
All is safely gathered in,
'Ere the winter storms begin.

So begins my favorite childhood Thanksgiving song written by Henry Alford in 1844. What is Thanksgiving to you? Is it turkey, stuffing, and cranberries? Or family, friends, and football? Or is it Pilgrims, Indians, and freedom?

There is a history in this feasting day, which is a proud American event. One where people celebrated the freedom they gained to worship in a way they believed to be true. One where people learned from and became friends with people of another culture. Pilgrims and Indians talked together, played games together, ate together, and gave thanks this first Thanksgiving celebration, which lasted three days.

Thanksgiving became a national holiday in the 19th century. In Sandra Markle's book, ***Exploring Autumn***, she explains: *"The current observance of a national Thanksgiving Day is largely the result of the thirty-year effort of Sarah Josepha Hale. As the editor of **Godey's Lady's Book**, a very popular publication in the United States, she campaigned for the establishment of this holiday. Finally, President Abraham Lincoln proclaimed that the last Thursday in November be set aside for this holiday, and the first official Thanksgiving Day was celebrated in 1863."*

The foods we associate with this meal are not necessarily the ones they ate in 1621. The Pilgrims ate what was near by, or food which they could grow in the rocky soil. The menu most probably included cod, sea bass, and possibly lobsters, clams, eels, and oysters from the ocean; wild turkey, duck, goose, and deer from the land; wild cranberries, currants, blueberries, cherries and raspberries, and carrots, turnips, radishes, onions, cabbages, and corn which they grew in the garden. In fact, deer meat was the featured main dish, rather than turkey, as it is today. Goat's milk was used to drink and make cheese instead of cow's, as this domestic animal did not arrive until 1625.

What would Thanksgiving be without pumpkin pie? Who else, besides pumpkin growers, would want to eat pumpkin pie in the spring or summer? Once a year seems to be just enough. Yet what else would you dream of eating when the chill in the air made you mindful of what lies ahead. The scent of cinnamon, cloves, ginger, the essence of pumpkin pie spice, fills the warmth of the kitchen, and you know you will be well fed.

When my older daughter, Emily, was preschool age, she didn't like many vegetables or fruits. And fruit pies were something she shied away from with a firm, "No, thank you." But there was something about pumpkin pie that made her try a bite and eat a whole piece. Maybe it was the texture, the smooth, spicy sweetness, and the whipped cream topping. She loved it! Children always keep me second-guessing because I never would have believed that pumpkin would have been the one pie Emily would eat.

People have tried modernizing pumpkin. They have made pumpkin ice cream and pumpkin cheesecake, pumpkin cookies, and pumpkin muffins, but the best way to serve pumpkin is baked in a pie. And pumpkin pie is relatively easy to make, even with children. After the pie crust is ready, all ingredients are mixed together in one bowl, poured into the crust and baked.

What makes up the filling of a pumpkin pie? ***The First American Cookbook—A Facsimile of American Cookery***, published in 1796 simply states: 'Pompkin (Pumpkin) No.2, One quart of milk, 1 pint pumpkin, 4 eggs, molaffes (molasses), allfpice (allspice), and ginger in a cruft (crust), bake 1 hour.'

Traditional Pumpkin Pie

1 unbaked 9-inch pie shell
2 cups (16 oz.) pumpkin
1 2/3 cups light cream
3/4 cup sugar
2 eggs
1/2 teaspoon cinnamon
1/4 teaspoon cloves
1/2 teaspoon ginger
1 /2 teaspoon salt

Have pie crust ready. Preheat oven to 425 degrees F.

Ask children to help measure and mix ingredients together in a large bowl. Pour into pie shell.

Bake for 15 minutes, then reduce heat to 350 degrees F and continue baking for 45 minutes or until set.

Cool. Serve each piece with a dollop of whipped cream.

Yield: 1 (9-inch) pie

Be sure to refrigerate your pie after it cools. Pumpkin pie is made with eggs, so it could spoil if left unrefrigerated.

Hot Fruit Compote

1 (16 oz.) can peach halves

1 (16 oz.) can pear halves

1 (16 oz.) can apricot halves

1 (8 oz.) can pineapple chunks

1/3 cup brown sugar

1/3 cup butter or margarine

1/2 teaspoon cinnamon

1/2 teaspoon ginger

1/4 teaspoon ground cloves

6 maraschino cherries, with stems

Drain and save juices from canned fruit. Reserve 1 1/2 cups of juice.

Children can layer canned fruits in 2-quart baking dish.

In a saucepan, melt butter or margarine; add brown sugar, spices, and the reserved juice. Heat and stir at low temperature until sugar is dissolved and mixture is hot. Spoon over fruit.

Bake in 350 degree F oven for 25 minutes.

Garnish with maraschino cherries, if desired.

Yield: 10 - 12 servings

No-Sugar Date Bars

1 cup dates

1 cup water

1/2 cup butter or margarine

2 eggs

1 teaspoon vanilla extract

1/2 cup chopped nuts

1 cup all-purpose flour

1 teaspoon baking soda

1/4 teaspoon salt

Children can use kitchen scissors to cut dates into small pieces. In medium saucepan, boil dates and water for 5 minutes. Add butter or margarine. Mix and set aside to cool.

Add eggs and vanilla to the date mixture in saucepan. Measure flour, baking soda, and salt. Add to mixture in pan. Stir in nuts.

Spread in greased 7 x 11-inch pan and bake in 350 degrees F oven for 20 - 25 minutes.

Yield: 15 bars

Variation for Spicy Date Bars: add 1/2 teaspoon cinnamon and 1/4 teaspoon nutmeg to flour mixture.

This is the time of year when we can take the time to appreciate how people lived and ate in days gone by. One way is by making homemade bread.

Company Refrigerator Rolls

Here is a recipe for rolls that children can help you make. The dough rises in the refrigerator overnight. The following day children can shape, bake, and eat their rolls for a special Thanksgiving treat! You will need to consider your time, as the rolls must rise about two to three hours before baking. The flavor and texture of these are wonderful!

1/2 cup warm water
1 package (2 1/2 teaspoons) yeast
1 teaspoon sugar
1 cup milk
1/3 cup butter *or* margarine
6 tablespoons sugar
2 teaspoons salt
1 egg *or* 2 egg whites
5 - 5 1/2 cups unbleached white flour

Pour the water into a small bowl. Test a drop on your wrist to see if it is just warm, not hot. Children can add the yeast, 1 teaspoon sugar, and stir. Set aside. Children can help measure and pour milk, butter or margarine, sugar, and salt into a saucepan. Heat just until butter or margarine melts. Remove from heat and let cool to lukewarm.

Pour milk mixture into a large bowl. Add softened yeast mixture. Children can add egg or egg whites, and 2 1/2 cups flour. Stir with a wooden spoon until smooth. Give everyone a turn. Continue adding enough flour to make a soft dough. You might need to stir, if it gets too difficult for the children.

Let the dough rest for 10 minutes. Then knead the dough on a floured board or cloth, by folding 1/3 of the dough towards you, pushing, and turning. Children will enjoy punching, pressing, and palming dough. Use enough flour to keep it from getting sticky. Continue kneading for about 10 minutes.

Place dough in a greased bowl and cover, or use a large (gallon-size) plastic bag. Zip or use twister tie, leaving enough room in the bag for dough to rise. Place in refrigerator overnight.

Shape rolls by cutting dough into 24 to 30 pieces. Children can shape into a ball or into a "snake" and then a knot, figure eight, braid, or other shape.

Place on a greased cookie sheet. Cover with a dishtowel; let rise 2 - 3 hours until almost doubled in bulk.

Bake in a preheated 375 degree F oven for 15 minutes or until golden brown.

Yield: about 2 dozen rolls

Special Sweet Potatoes and Apple Casserole

This sweet potato recipe is a welcome change from the marshmallow variety.

4 sweet potatoes
4 cooking apples
1/4 cup butter or margarine
1/4 cup sugar
1/2 cup orange juice
2 tablespoons almonds, sliced

Boil sweet potatoes in salted water to cover, until tender, about 30 minutes. Then cool. Children can remove skins and slice. Pare, core, and slice apples.

Preheat oven to 350 degrees F. Melt butter or margarine in a small saucepan. Add sugar and orange juice. Bring to a boil, then remove from heat. *Use caution, as this syrup mixture gets very hot.*

Children can layer the sweet potatoes and apples in a 3-quart casserole. Pour the sauce on top. Sprinkle with almonds.

Bake for 30 minutes, or until apples are tender.

Yield: 8 - 10 servings

Green Bean Bake

1 package (10 oz.) French cut green beans, frozen
1 (10 oz.) can cream of mushroom soup
1 (8 oz.) can sliced water chestnuts, drained
1 teaspoon soy sauce
1 (3 oz.) can French fried onions

Partially cook frozen green beans according to directions.

In 1 1/2-quart baking dish, children can mix beans with cream of mushroom soup, water chestnuts, and soy sauce.

Bake in 350 degree F oven for 12 - 15 minutes or until bubbly.

Sprinkle with French fried onions and bake an additional 5 minutes or until brown.

Yield: 6 - 8 servings

Favorite Cranberry Salad

This wonderful cranberry salad can be made the day before.

1/2 envelope unflavored gelatin
1/4 cup cold water
1 (6-oz) cherry gelatin
2 cups hot water
1 tablespoon lemon juice
1 cup crushed pineapple, drained
Juice from drained pineapple
    plus cold water to make 1 cup
2 cups raw cranberries
1 orange with peel
1 cup chopped celery
1 cup chopped pecans or walnuts

Soften unflavored gelatin in cold water. Dissolve cherry gelatin in hot water. Children can stir with a wooden spoon. Add unflavored gelatin; stir. Add lemon juice and pineapple juice mixture. Pour into a 9 x 12-inch glass pan. Chill until partially set, about 1/2 hour.

In the meanwhile, finely chop cranberries and orange in food processor or blender. Prepare celery and walnuts. Children can add pineapple, cranberries, orange, celery, and nuts to gelatin. Stir to combine.

Chill until set. To serve, cut into squares and serve on lettuce.

Yield: 12 servings

Twenty-Four Hour Fruit Salad

1 (16-oz.) can chunk pineapple
1 (17-oz) can white or Bing cherries
2 (11-oz.) cans mandarin oranges
2 cups miniature marshmallows
1 cup whipping cream, whipped

Dressing:
2 eggs
2 tablespoons sugar
2 tablespoons pineapple juice
1 tablespoon vinegar
1 tablespoon lemon juice
Dash of salt
1 tablespoon butter

Drain fruits. Children can combine fruits and marshmallows in large bowl.

Meanwhile, in a small bowl, make dressing by beating eggs with rotary beater until light in color and foamy. Pour into small saucepan and add sugar, pineapple juice, vinegar, lemon juice, and salt. Cook over low heat, stirring constantly, just to boiling. Add butter. Cool.

Fold in 1 cup whipping cream. Pour over fruit mixture, mixing gently. Spoon into clear glass bowl, cover with plastic wrap, and refrigerate for 24 hours.

Yield: 8 - 10 servings

The Legend of the Five Kernels

Have you heard of the legend of the five kernels? This legend is about the Pilgrims. The first winter the Pilgrims almost starved. It was very cold, and they did not have enough food. Some days they had little to eat, and had to split what they had among many people. Some days they ate only five kernels of corn. But the spring came, and the Pilgrims planted, hunted, and fished. The next winter there was more food, but they always put five kernels of corn on the table to remind them of how much they had.

A friend gave us a gift of this legend printed on a small piece of paper and included five kernels of candy corn, complete in a zip-lock snack bag. This was a wonderful way for us to recall the many blessings we had received during the year.

You can ask your child, "What are you thankful for?" Each kernel can remind you of one thing for which to be thankful. Together you can decide what each kernel symbolizes.

To give to a friend, enclose these reminders, either hand written or typed, in the bag, along with five kernels. Here are the reminders my friend wrote to me:

The first kernel reminds us of the beauty of autumn.
The second kernel reminds us of the love in our family.
The third kernel reminds us of God's love.
The fourth kernel reminds us of our friendships.
The fifth kernel reminds us of freedom.

Happy Thanksgiving!

WINTER IDEAS

• For Hanukkah, talk to your child about why latkes (potato pancakes) are eaten during this time. Discuss different ways to make potatoes.

• For Christmas, check out a cookbook from the library with recipes used by your ancestors. Make a traditional cookie or bread recipe from that country.

• For Kwanzaa, paint a basket black, and place red and green apples in it. The traditional colors of Kwanzaa are black, red, and green.

• For New Year's Day, ask your child what food he or she thinks will bring good luck for the new year. Eat that food on New Year's Day.

• For Valentine's Day, help your child make heart-shaped sandwiches using a cookie cutter.

• For President's Day, discuss the lives of Abraham Lincoln and George Washington at the dinner table.

• For St. Patrick's Day, read an after-dinner story about a leprechaun.

Have a Cookie-Baking or Exchange Party

Winifred Laber bakes a certain molasses cookie every year at Christmas. The cookies hold a special memory for her father, which was passed on to her.

"My Dad, Keith Anderson, served in Europe during WWII, and his mother, Mabel, would make these cookies and ship them out," said Wini. "The spices aged and the cookies softened in the month it took for the box to arrive in England, Wales or Germany. My Dad always said, in later years, the ones he received overseas tasted better than the fresh baked ones."

She added, "But maybe it was more than the aged spices. Those cookies were a little piece of home to a 19 year old far from home in the middle of a world war."

Memories and baking traditional cookies are a big part of the Christmas season. A fun way to get together with friends and get something done is by having a cookie-baking or exchange party. You can share recipes and treasured memories of baking when you were growing up.

Cookie-Baking Party

Have the cookie dough made beforehand, and invite your guests to bring dough as well. Plan for a day or evening when you and other friends are available. Kids can join in the fun. The younger the child, the more help you will need to give.

Use the cookie recipes found in this section, or use an old family favorite. Children will have the most fun with dough they can hold, mold, and decorate. You can choose a healthy vegetable or fruit based cookie, or decide to splurge with butter creams. Whatever you choose, be sure to send a container home with each person who comes.

After making the cookies, have drinks on hand. Sample the finished product. Fresh fruits and cheeses can add to the snack, and extend the quantity of cookies, which can then be tucked away for a special guest or holiday. Thank your guests for coming to help. If it turns out to be a good day and a good memory, you might make this activity into a family tradition.

Cookie Exchange

In a cookie exchange, each family brings several dozen cookies, and then exchanges them with the other families who attend. When several families come, you take home a wide assortment of cookies. The host or hostess of the party decides a set number of cookies to bring, such as six dozen. Favorite holiday cookies are baked a day or so before the cookie exchange date.

At the party, each family places their container of cookies on a table. Children can stand by their container, holding a tray or extra container in hand. The host or hostess signals to start. It is fun for children to choose the cookies as they walk around the table, taking a cookie from each container until all the cookies are gone.

If you brought six dozen cookies, you will take home a variety of six dozen. Of course, you will be taking home some of your own cookies. And what a lovely assortment you will have to share with your family and serve your guests!

Holiday Candy Cane Cookies

1/2 cup butter, softened
1/2 cup shortening
1 cup confectioners' sugar
1 teaspoon vanilla
1 1/2 teaspoons almond extract
1 egg
2 1/2 cups flour
1 teaspoon salt
1/2 teaspoon red food coloring
1/4 cup crushed peppermint candy
1/4 cup granulated sugar

Preheat oven to 375 degrees F. Children can help measure butter, shortening, confectioners' sugar, vanilla, almond extract, and crack egg into large mixing bowl. Children can mix with large wooden spoon or adult can beat with electric mixer until well mixed. *Note: there is no baking powder in this recipe.*

Stir in flour and salt. Divide dough in half. Add red food coloring to one half of dough. Pinch off about a teaspoon of red dough. Children can shape into about a 4-inch rope by rolling back and forth on lightly floured board or cloth. Repeat with plain dough. Set side-by-side and twist together. Place on ungreased baking sheet, curving one end down to form handle of cane.

Repeat process, placing candy canes about 2-inches apart on baking sheet. Bake for 9 minutes, until very light brown. Meanwhile, mix peppermint candy and sugar. Sprinkle on cookies right when they come out of the oven. Then remove to cooling rack.

Yield: about 4 dozen cookies

Basic Cookie Dough and Variations

This basic dough can be used to make two kinds of molded cookies, perfect for little fingers.

1/3 cup shortening
1/3 cup butter
3/4 cup sugar
1 egg
1 teaspoon vanilla
1 3/4 cup white _or_
   1 1/2 cups whole wheat flour
1 teaspoon baking powder
1/2 teaspoon salt

Children can help measure and stir. Blend shortening, butter, and sugar. Add egg and vanilla. Stir in flour, baking powder, and salt.

Refrigerate dough for later use, or use right away. Divide dough to make variations.

Variation #1 Sugar Cookies
Preheat oven to 375 degrees F. Use 1/2 of dough. On a floured surface, roll dough to 1/8-inch. Children can help cut with cookie-cutter; place on ungreased baking sheet and sprinkle with colored sugar, if desired.

Bake about 6 minutes or until light brown.

Yield: about 3 dozen cookies

Variation #2 Cinnamon Circles
In a cereal bowl, children can mix 2 teaspoons sugar and 2 teaspoons cinnamon; set aside. Use 1/2 of dough. Children can mold a rounded teaspoon of dough into a ball, then roll in cinnamon mixture.

Place 2-inches apart on ungreased cookie sheet. Bake at 375 degrees F for 8 - 10 minutes.

Yield: about 2 dozen cookies

Favorite Molasses Cookies

2 1/2 cups flour
2 teaspoons baking soda
1 teaspoon salt
1/2 teaspoon ground cloves
1 teaspoon ground cinnamon
1 teaspoon ground ginger
3/4 cup shortening
1 cup brown sugar
1 egg
4 tablespoons molasses
White sugar

Children can sift flour, soda, salt, and spices together. Set aside. Mix shortening, brown sugar, egg, and molasses. Add dry ingredients gradually. Children will have fun rolling and forming them into balls the size of walnuts.

Roll in sugar and place on a platter and chill one hour, then bake on a cookie sheet at 350 degrees F for 8 - 10 minutes. Remove from cookie sheet and let cool on rack.

Yield: 5 dozen cookies

Note: Best when aged a few weeks.

Wheat-Free Peanut Butter Cookies

For those with wheat allergies and others — here is an easy, yummy peanut butter cookie made without flour.

1 cup creamy peanut butter
1 cup sugar
1 large egg
1 teaspoon vanilla

Preheat oven to 325 degrees F.

Children can help measure and stir together all ingredients in a medium-sized bowl. Using two teaspoons, scoop and drop dough onto ungreased cookie sheet.

Flatten with tines of fork. Dip fork into flour if needed, to keep from sticking to dough.

Bake for 15 to 18 minutes, or until lightly browned. Remove cookies from cookie sheet and cool on a rack.

Yield: 3 dozen cookies

Amy's Cranberry Oatmeal Cookies

Note from Amy: *Oatmeal cookies are my favorite. I love the wholesome goodness of oats, and the chewy texture they add to cookies. When I discovered the sweet flavor of dried cranberries, I added them to my oatmeal cookie recipe, in place of raisins.*

3/4 cup butter, softened
1 1/4 cups firmly packed brown sugar
1 egg
1/3 cup milk <u>or</u> water
1 1/2 teaspoons vanilla
3 cups quick (1 minute) rolled oats
1 cup all-purpose flour
1/2 teaspoon baking soda
1/2 teaspoon salt
1/4 teaspoon cinnamon
1 cup sweetened dried cranberries
1 cup chopped walnuts

Cream butter and sugar. Beat in egg, milk, and vanilla.

Children can add rolled oats, flour, baking soda, salt, and cinnamon. Stir in dried cranberries and walnuts.

Drop teaspoonfuls of dough 2-inches apart on greased cookie sheets. Bake at 375 degrees F for 10 - 12 minutes or until light brown. Let cool 1 minute on cookie sheet then remove to cooling racks to cool completely.

Yield: about 3 dozen cookies

Variation for Chocolate Chip Oatmeal Cookies: replace dried cranberries with chocolate chips.

Variation for Raisin Studded Oatmeal Cookies: replace dried cranberries with raisins.

Date-Coconut Balls

1 cup dates, cut in pieces
1 cup coconut
2 eggs, beaten
3/4 cup sugar
1 teasoon vanilla
1/4 teaspoon almond flavoring
1 cup nuts

Children can use kitchen scissors to cut dates into small pieces. In medium bowl, add cut-up dates and coconut. In another small bowl, children can beat eggs, then add to dates and coconut. Mix in sugar, flavorings, and nuts. Spoon into greased casserole.

Bake at 350 degrees F for 25 - 30 minutes. Stir occasionally while cooling. After mixture is cool enough to handle, shape into small balls and roll in white sugar.

Yield: about 2 dozen cookies

Jelly-Belly Cookies

1/4 cup butter
1/4 cup shortening
1/4 cup brown sugar
1 egg, separated
1/2 teaspoon vanilla
1 cup flour
1/4 teaspoon salt
3/4 cup finely chopped nuts
Red jelly or jam, such as
  strawberry or raspberry

Preheat oven to 350 degrees F. Grease cookie sheet. Wash hands thoroughtly; make sure finger nails are extra clean for this recipe.

Children can help measure butter, shortening, and brown sugar into a medium-sized bowl; beat until fluffy. Separate white and yolk of egg by cracking the egg in half and transferring the yolk from one half of the shell to the other, while allowing the white to fall into a bowl beneath the egg. Add yolk to butter mixture; mix to combine. Reserve egg white.

Stir vanilla into butter mixture. Stir in flour and salt. This makes a stiff dough. *(Note: there is no baking powder in this recipe.)* Children can roll and press teaspoonfuls of dough into 1-inch balls. Beat egg white slightly. Dip each ball into egg white; use a fork to drain excess egg white from dough. Then roll in chopped nuts.

Place on cookie sheet. Children can press thumb into center of cookie, making a deep well, enough for a teaspoon of jelly. Be sure to wash hands before as well as afterward, as raw egg can carry bacteria.

Bake 10 minutes, or until lightly browned. Remove cookies from baking sheet to cooling rack. Cool, then fill thumb indentation with jelly or jam.

Yield: 2 dozen cookies

Simple Holiday Gifts From the Kitchen

I heard a knock at the kitchen door and wondered who would be out on this blustery cold day. I set down my mug of tea and pulled my cardigan tight around my waist, bracing myself as I opened the door. My neighbor smiled and looked down at her son. He beamed with pride as he handed me a tin heavy with baked goods. As I thanked him and invited them in, I felt all the good will of the season, the joy of giving, and the joy of receiving gifts made with one's hands.

Giving simple gifts from your kitchen can be very rewarding. Children can help with the creation, the packaging, and the delivery. This way you can help your family know that what is important is time together, the capability to create, and the desire to give and share.

Guidelines for making gifts
- keep it simple
- label your gift
- include the recipe, if applicable
- decorate your gift with a bow
- when making a gift with a child, expect an imperfect product
- deliver your gift with your child present

Here are suggestions for easy gifts from the kitchen.

Honey Butter

Great as a toast topper!

1/2 cup butter or margarine, softened
1/2 cup honey
1 small (1 cup size) empty butter or margarine tub
Ribbon

Cream together the margarine or butter and honey using a wooden spoon. Children can spoon honey butter in butter or margarine tub. Label. Tie with a ribbon.

Yield: 1 cup

Note: children under one year of age should not eat honey.

Tea Tin

Variety of teas: imported, herbal, and flavored
Pretty tin
Children can fill a small, pretty tin with your favorite tea. Tie with a ribbon.

*Variation: For Coffee Basket, buy small packets of gourmet coffee. Use a basket
instead of a tin. Tie a ribbon on the handle.*

Fruit Basket

Variety of fruit
Unshelled nuts
Large basket or sturdy cardboard circle, about 15 inches, covered with aluminum foil

Children will enjoy choosing fruit to include in the basket. The largest, most beautiful apples, pears,
and oranges are available at this time of year. They look lovely as gifts. Pick whatever is available in
your store. Do not wash the fruit before making your arrangement, as it will spoil faster if washed.
Take all the fruit and place it on a table near the basket or cardboard. Children can arrange the fruit
any way they like. For cardboard, arrange the fruit in one layer. For a basket, add a second layer of
fruit. Bananas add a pleasing color and shape to the arrangement. Place unshelled nuts in the spaces
between the fruit. Cover all with plastic wrap and add a big bow. Deliver as soon as possible or keep
in a cool (not freezing) place.

Hearty Soup Mix

1 package mixed bean soup mix
1 pint glass jar
*Scrap of cloth cut into a
    circle 1/2 inch wider than the
    opening of the jar*
Ribbon, about 18 inches
Recipe card

Children can pour bean soup mix into glass jar. Place cloth
on top and tie with ribbon.

Copy recipe from package for mixed bean soup onto recipe
card. Attach to jar.

Yield: 1 jar

Holiday Spice Mix

This spice mix will add a festive, warm, welcoming flavor to apple cider, and apple and cranberry juice.

1 cinnamon stick
1 teaspoon ground cinnamon
1 teaspoon whole allspice
1 teaspoon whole cloves
1/2 teaspoon ground ginger
1/2 teaspoon ground nutmeg
Two 6-inch squares of cheesecloth

Children can collect and measure all spices. Place them in the center of two 6-inch square pieces of cheesecloth (double thickness). Bring corners together and tie with dental floss. Add another ribbon of a bright color and give spice mix to a special friend.

Add a note: *"Drop one bag of spice mix in 4 cups hot apple cider, or apple or cranberry juice. Let it brew for 10 minutes and serve. Smell the aroma, taste, and enjoy!"*

Yield: 2 gifts

Chocolate Chip Cookies in a Jar

This is an attractive gift, with the layered ingredients clearly visible through the glass jar.

1/2 cup white sugar
1 cup semi-sweet chocolate chips
1/2 cup brown sugar
1 1/2 cups flour
1/2 teaspoon baking soda
1/2 teaspoon salt
1 wide-mouth quart glass jar
Scrap of cloth cut into a
  circle 1/2 inch wider than the
  opening of the jar
Ribbon, about 18 inches
Recipe card

Children can help layer and pack the ingredients in the order listed; pack down brown sugar.

If you have extra space at the top, you can add nuts or more chocolate chips. Screw on lid.

Place fabric scrap over lid. Tie with a ribbon.

Yield: 1 jar

Copy the following directions onto a recipe card and attach to jar:

Directions for Chocolate Chip Cookies

Preheat oven to 375 degrees F. Empty contents into a bowl. Stir in 2/3 cup of softened butter, 1 egg, and 1 teaspoon vanilla. Mix thoroughly. Drop by teaspoonfuls onto an ungreased baking sheet. Bake for 8 - 10 minutes. *Yield: about 3 dozen cookies*

Baked Goods

You can make traditional recipes for cookies, cakes, and breads, or buy packaged dough to bake and decorate. It depends on how much time and energy you have, and what you want to do. Arrange an assortment on a plate or place in a tin. Use a doily for a fancy, old-fashioned look. Add a candy cane for color. Cover with plastic wrap and tie with a ribbon.

Carrot-Raisin Bread

This recipe stays moist and is full of nutritious ingredients.

2 cups shredded carrots

3 eggs

1 cup vegetable oil

1/3 cup water

2 teaspoons grated orange peel

1 1/3 cups sugar

1 teaspoon vanilla

3 cups flour

2 teaspoons baking soda

1 teaspoon baking powder

1 teaspoon salt

1 teaspoon cinnamon

1 teaspoon cloves

2/3 cup chopped nuts

2/3 cup raisins

Preheat oven to 350 degrees F. Children can grease and flour two 9 x 5-inch loaf pans.

Shred carrots in food processor or by hand with a grater. Children can beat eggs, oil, water, carrots, orange peel, sugar, and vanilla with a wire whisk or wooden spoon.

In a separate bowl, sift or stir flour, baking soda, baking powder, salt, cinnamon, and cloves. Add to carrot mixture just until all ingredients are moistened. Add nuts and raisins. Spread in pans.

Bake 1 hour. Cool 10 minutes. Turn out of pans. Freezes well.

Yield: 2 loaves

Variations: Substitute the following uncooked fruit and vegetables for the 2 cups shredded carrots in the recipe above:
Apple Bread: 2 cups chopped, unpeeled apples
Zucchini Bread: 2 cups shredded zucchini
Sweet Potato Bread: 2 cups peeled and shredded sweet potato, 1/2 cup shredded coconut, and 1/4 cup water

Remember the Birds

Take some time to remember the birds. During the winter season, it is harder for the birds to find food. A gift you can give them, or to a bird-lover, is a pinecone bird feeder. Tie a string or piece of yarn around a pinecone. Children can spread peanut butter on the pinecone and roll in birdseed. Hang from a tree branch near a window where you can watch. Give them water, too, if possible.

A Multicultural Celebration

Bing Boettner celebrated Christmas in the Philippines much the same as in the United States, but there were some distinctive differences. "In the Philippines, when I go caroling door to door, there is an unspoken request for money for the church," she said.

After marrying an American and moving to the mid-western United States, Bing misses the large extended family gatherings she attended as a child when roasted pig on a spit, complete with an apple in its mouth, was holiday fare in the warm weather of the islands. She laughs about her pillow case "stocking," explaining the bigger the "stocking" the more presents she received!

The winter holidays are perhaps the most anticipated, most prepared for, and most loved by people around the world. Several joyous holidays are celebrated in December: Christmas, the Christian celebration of the birth of Jesus Christ, Hanukkah, the Jewish holiday of the Festival of Lights, and a relatively new holiday, Kwanzaa, an African-American celebration, inspired by African traditions.

The Christian holiday of Christmas, December 25, is celebrated with a variety of traditions. Christians from many countries have special days to celebrate the birth of Jesus.

One of the many traditions for Christmas from Mexico is Las Posadas, which means "the inns." A parade of people knock on doors to see if there is any room at the "inn" for Mary to have her baby. Acting out this story by knocking on doors is one way children can understand the Christmas message. On each of the nine nights of Las Posadas, which ends on Christmas Eve, children have the opportunity to hit a piñata, a clay or paper maché animal filled with gifts and candy.

Food plays a large part in most holiday celebrations. Many cultures have foods made just at Christmas time, especially breads, cakes, candies, and cookies. This December, when your family gathers for the winter holidays, why not have a multicultural celebration by adding some new dishes to your menu, along with the special, traditional foods you usually prepare?

Easy Chocolate Fudge

1 (7-oz.) jar marshmallow creme
1 (12-oz.) bag semi-sweet
  chocolate chips
1 cup chopped walnuts (optional)

Butter an 8 x 8-inch square pan. Set aside.

In a medium-sized saucepan, melt marshmallow creme and chocolate chips in a bowl in the microwave oven, or melt in a double boiler over hot water, stirring constantly.

When chips are melted, add nuts and pour into prepared pan. Cool. Cut into 1-inch square pieces.

Yield: 1 pound

Mexican Salad

With all the calorie-laden foods associated with the season, a refreshing, healthful salad is a welcome addition to a holiday meal. This salad is traditionally served after Christmas Eve Mass.

1 head iceberg lettuce
4 bananas
8 small cooked beets
4 oranges
3 limes
4 apples
2 (16 oz.) cans pineapple chunks
Seeds of 2 pomegranates
1 cup salted peanuts
1/4 cup sugar (optional)
1/2 cup salad oil
1/4 cup cider vinegar

Children can help prepare all vegetables and fruits. They can core, tear, and rinse lettuce. Slice bananas and beets. Peel and slice oranges and limes. Leave peel on, but core and slice apples. Coarsely chop peanuts.

Place lettuce in a large serving bowl. Place the fruits and vegetables on top, leaving pomegranate seeds and peanuts to add last. Sprinkle with sugar, if desired.

Mix oil and vinegar and pour over all just before serving.

Yield: 8 - 10 servings

The Jewish religion celebrates the eight days of Hanukkah, which usually falls in the month of December. This celebration recalls the Jewish victory over their much stronger oppressors who had tried to stamp out their religion. When the Jews recaptured their temple in Jerusalem, and in the process of purifying the temple, a one-day's supply of oil lasted eight days until more purified oil arrived.

Observances include lighting one candle on the menorah on each of the eight days, saying blessings, singing songs, and gift-giving. One traditional food for Hanukkah is latkes, which are pancakes, made with grated potatoes and onion, and fried in oil. This is to remind the Jewish people about the great miracle.

Potato Latkes (Pancakes)

These latkes are a delicious reminder of the miracle. They are often served with applesauce.

4 potatoes
1 onion
1 teaspoon salt
1 beaten egg
3 tablespoons flour
1/2 teaspoon baking powder
1/4 cup oil
Applesauce

Pare and grate potatoes by hand or in a food processor. Drain by pressing in a sieve or colander. Grate onion.

Mix potatoes, onion, salt, egg, flour, and baking powder. Heat oil in a large skillet over medium heat.

Adults will need to fry spoonfuls of the potato mixture until brown on both sides. Drain. Serve with applesauce.

Yield: serves 4

Guidelines for Cooking Potato Latkes

- Fry until brown, and potatoes are cooked through.
- Add oil, as needed, in-between batches.
- Sprinkle with salt after cooking.
- Try sour cream as an alternative to applesauce.
- Potato latkes are so filling, they can be served as a main dish.

The celebration of Kwanzaa was created in America in 1966 by Dr. Maulana Karenga when he was teaching at California State University. The word "Kwanzaa" is Swahili for "first fruits." This non-religious observance is a time of recommitment and renewal, signifying the cultural connection between African-Americans and Africa. A candle is lit and a principle of black culture is discussed each evening for seven evenings beginning on December 26. This coincides with the African "festival of the harvest of the first crops." Traditional colors for Kwanzaa are black, red, and green.

African Vegetable Stew

Gifts and a dinner of African food, such as this vegetable stew, are also a part of Kwanza.

2 tablespoon oil
1 onion, chopped
1 clove garlic, minced
2 yams, scrubbed with a
  vegetable brush and rinsed,
  and sliced thick
1/2 cup raisins
1 (16-oz.) can garbanzo beans
  (chick peas)
1 (16-oz.) can tomatoes
Salt and pepper to taste
Hot pepper sauce
Cooked rice

Heat oil over medium heat in large pot. Add onion and garlic; fry a few minutes until onion is transparent. Children can help add yams, raisins, garbanzos, and tomatoes to the pot.

Simmer over low heat about 30 minutes, or until yams are tender and flavors are blended. Add salt, pepper, and hot pepper sauce to taste.

Serve over rice.

Yield: 4 - 6 servings

Seven Principles of Black Culture

1) unity (umoja)
2) self-determination (kujichagulia)
3) collective work and responsibility (ujima)
4) cooperative economics (ujamaa)
5) purpose (nia)
6) creativity (kuumba)
7) faith (imani)

Planning a New Year's Open House

New Year's Day is a time of *open house.* It is a time when people come to visit. This custom dates back to olden days when people traveled in a horse and carriage to several friends' homes, sampling cake, cookies, or other holiday specialties. During these gatherings, children were asked to hop and jump around the table before being allowed to take a cookie. The little *dance* was supposed to insure good luck for the coming year.

While different cultures celebrate with different foods, the goal is similar–to welcome the New Year by visiting with friends and family. The following recipes help you start out the New Year with food appropriate for the season. They are offered with the hope of bringing you good health and cheer for the New Year!

Jumping Jill Cookies

1 cup butter
1 1/2 cups white sugar
2 eggs
1 teaspoon vanilla
2 3/4 cups sifted flour
1 teaspoon baking soda
2 teaspoons cream of tartar
1 /2 teaspoon salt
2 tablespoons sugar
1 tablespoon cinnamon

Cream the butter; add the 1 1/2 cups of sugar gradually, beating until light and creamy.

Add eggs one at a time, beating until just incorporated. Add vanilla. Children can stir in the flour, baking soda, cream of tartar, and salt.

Chill the dough in the refrigerator for 2 hours.

Preheat oven to 375 degrees F.

In a small bowl, stir together the 2 tablespoons of sugar and 1 tablespoon cinnamon. Children can roll the dough into 1-inch balls and roll in the sugar/cinnamon mixture.

Place on a greased cookie sheet, 2 inches apart; press dough lightly with the tines of a fork.

Bake for 10 minutes or until light brown.

Yield: 6 dozen cookies

Good-Luck Black-Eyed Peas

In the American South, people serve black-eyed peas and corn bread to bring good luck. Soak the peas the night before.

*1 pound package dried
  black-eyed peas
1 ham hock*

Children can place peas in a 4-quart pot; cover peas with water. Let set overnight. Drain water and cover with fresh water. Add the ham hock and bring to a boil. Turn down heat and let simmer, covered, for two to three hours, until peas are tender. Check occasionally and add additional water, if necessary.

Adult will need to remove ham hock from pot. Separate the ham from the bones and fat. Put the ham back in the pot and discard the bones and fat. Serve in soup bowls with corn bread on the side.

Yield: 8 servings

Crusty Corn Bread

*1 1/4 cups flour
3/4 cup white corn meal
1/4 cup sugar
2 teaspoons baking powder
1 /2 teaspoon salt
1 cup milk
1/4 cup vegetable oil
1 egg, beaten*

Preheat oven to 400 degrees F. Grease an 8 or 9-inch square pan.

Children can measure flour, corn meal, sugar, baking powder, and salt into a medium-sized bowl.

Make a well in the center and add milk, oil, and egg. Mix just until dry ingredients are moistened, about 50 strokes.

Pour into prepared pan. Bake 20 - 25 minutes or until light brown. Cut into 9 squares. Best served warm with plenty of butter.

Yield: 9 servings

Parmesan Spinach Dip

1 (10 oz.) package frozen chopped spinach, thawed
1 (14 oz.) can artichoke hearts, packed in water
1 clove garlic, minced
1/3 to 1/2 cup mayonnaise or salad dressing
1/2 cup grated Parmesan cheese

Preheat oven to 350 degrees. F.

Defrost frozen spinach several hours beforehand, or microwave on full power for about 4 minutes. Children can help press spinach in colander or sieve to remove excess liquid.

Drain artichoke hearts and chop fine. Mince garlic. Children can mix spinach, artichoke, garlic, mayonnaise, and Parmesan cheese in a 2-quart casserole. Bake 20 minutes. Serve warm with crackers.

Yield: 4 cups

Cheddar Cheese Ball

A cheese ball is always a welcome addition at a party.

4 cups shredded Cheddar cheese
2 (3-oz.) cream cheese, softened
1/3 cup mayonnaise
1 teaspoon Worcestershire sauce
1/8 teaspoon each: onion salt, garlic salt, celery salt
1/3 cup minced fresh parsley

Children can measure and stir together all ingredients except parsley. Chill slightly.

Shape into ball. Roll in parsley. Cover and chill until ready to use. Serve with crackers.

Yield: 1 cheese ball

Hot Cinnamon Apple Cider

This cider warms anyone coming in from the cold, and is enjoyed by parents and children alike.

2 quarts apple cider or apple juice
1/2 cup brown sugar
1 stick cinnamon
6 whole cloves
Cinnamon sticks or orange wedges for garnish

Children can measure and place all ingredients in large saucepan. Heat slowly to simmering. Cover pan and simmer 20 minutes. Strain out spices.

Serve in mugs with a cinnamon stick or orange wedge. Make sure it is warm, not hot, for children to drink.

Yield: 16 servings

When having an open house, fancy hors d'oeuvres are perfect. Children can choose a base, topping, and garnish. Place on a platter and refrigerate until serving.

Bases
- cucumber slice
- honeydew cube
- mini-sized bread
- toast, cut into triangles
  or cut with cookie cutter

Toppings
- cream cheese
- Cheddar or Swiss cheese
- tuna or chicken salad
- ham slice

Garnish
- olive and/or pickle slices
- cherry, halved
- frilly toothpick

A Valentine's Day Tea Party

My daughter, Sarah, smiled and said, "This is the best sandwich I've ever tasted!"
"Thank you for helping me make it," I said.
What I was thinking was: I love you, and I love cooking with you. I love watching you smile, your joy, the fun you have. I love watching your sensory experience and the wonder in your eyes.

Valentine's Day, February 14, is a time when we can celebrate the love of parent and child, and of families and friends. Talk to your child about the Valentine colors of red, pink and white. Tell them about the Valentine symbols of hearts, cupids with arrows, and doves. Show them how to show love: hold hands, hug, and kiss.

Getting Ready for a Valentine's Day Tea Party

Placemats

Red construction paper
Lace doilies
Heart stickers
Cupids, doves, or other symbols of love
Glue
Clear contact paper

Preparation: Place a layer of newspapers on your work surface. Set out one piece of red construction paper per child attending. Have the doilies, stickers, and symbols in the center of the table.
At the party: Supervise children as they glue items to their place mats. They can write their name and the date, or you can write it for them. Protect with clear contact paper.

The Table

Preparation: Make a centerpiece to set a traditional romantic mood, such as satin, lace, hearts, rings, doves, etc. One idea is to involve your child in decorating a basket. Tie on satin ribbon and lace bows. Entwine fresh or silk flowers. Glue on paper hearts and paper doves. Keep Valentine cards in the basket. Use a white, pink, or red tablecloth; place centerpiece on the table.

At the party: When the placemats are completed, add them to your table setting.

Menu for Valentine's Day Party

Love Potion Punch
Queen of Hearts Tea Sandwiches
Apple Arrows

Love Potion Punch

Use any red juice, such as cranberry
Serve with ice

Queen of Hearts Tea Sandwiches

Cream cheese, softened
Any red jam or fruit spread,
* such as strawberry, red*
* raspberry, or cherry*
Bread
Heart shaped cookie cutter

To soften cream cheese, leave at room temperature about an hour before preparing recipe, or microwave for 2 minutes on defrost power.

Children can stir together 2 parts cream cheese to 1 part jam or fruit spread. For example, blend 2 tablespoons cream cheese to 1 tablespoon strawberry jam.

The cream cheese mixture should turn a beautiful pink. Children can spread the mixture on bread with a butter knife.

Cut with a heart-shaped cookie cutter. Use a butter knife to separate the bread from the cookie cutter. The number of tea sandwiches depends on the size of your cookie cutter. A one-inch heart cuts 4 hearts from one slice of bread.

Place on a pretty plate. Make some hearts with only cream cheese, and some spread with only jelly or fruit spread. Refrigerate until ready to serve.

Apple Arrows

Rinse, core, and slice apples into 8 wedges. Dip in lemon juice to prevent turning brown. Let your child help you place slices next to or around Queen of Hearts Tea Sandwiches.

Party Game

A-Tisket A-Tasket

A tisket a-tasket
a red and yellow basket
I wrote a Valentine to my love
and on the way I dropped it,
I dropped it, I dropped it,
and on the way I dropped it.
I wrote a letter to my love
and on the way I dropped it.

Friends sit in a circle on the floor in an area where there is enough room to run around the circle. Everyone sings this song while one child walks around the circle with a red and yellow basket with a Valentine card in his hand.

He drops the Valentine behind one person, who must jump up and run after him around the circle, until the child sits down in the empty space. Then it is the second person's turn to walk around the circle while everyone sings. Repeat until everyone has had a least one turn, or until everyone is tired of playing.

Variations of A-Tisket A-Tasket

• Change the words in the rhyme to fit the color of your basket.
• Use a felt heart instead of a Valentine card.
• Use a heart-shaped beanbag instead of a card.

The following are other food suggestions for Valentine's Day:

Valentine Sandwiches

1 cup ground cooked ham
1/2 cup grated carrot
1/2 cup mayonnaise
1 1/2 teaspoon prepared
  horseradish

Sandwich bread
Butter, softened

Children can mix together ground cooked ham and grated carrot with mayonnaise and prepared horseradish. (Adult may need to grate the carrot.)

Children can cut small hearts with heart-shaped cookie cutter from center of half the bread slices. Spread hearts with softened butter. On the whole slices of bread, spread the ham mixture. Place bread hearts on whole bread slices to serve.

Dry the bread pieces remaining from the heart cut-outs in a low temperature oven. Use to make bread crumbs, or give the birds a treat and feed the bread left-overs to them.

Red Salad

Make any strawberry or raspberry red gelatin salad following directions on the package. Add fruit, such as bananas or canned crushed pineapple. Spoon into individual heart molds. Chill until firm.

Meringue Hearts

3 egg whites
1 teaspoon vanilla
1/4 teaspoon cream of tartar
Dash of salt
3/4 cup sugar
Red food coloring
1 quart vanilla ice cream
1 (10 oz.) package frozen
  strawberries in their juice

Beat egg whites with vanilla, cream of tartar, and salt until frothy. Gradually add sugar, small amounts at a time, until stiff peaks form. Add red food coloring to give meringue a light pink tint.

Children can cut heart pattern from 4-inch square of paper. Cover baking sheet with brown paper. Trace 6 hearts from pattern onto brown paper. Children can help spread meringue over each heart shape, making each 1/4 inch thick.

Bake in preheated 275 degrees F oven for 1 hour. Turn off heat and let dry in oven overnight. When ready to serve, fill meringues with scoops of vanilla ice cream and top with strawberries.

Yield: 6 heart meringues

President's Day

A centerpiece of a bowl of pennies and quarters, which show the profile of these much loved and respected presidents, is perfect for President's Day. Having a penny or quarter hunt is a fun activity at this time of year. Parents can hide the money and children find and keep it, or divide accordingly.

The birthdays of two American presidents, George Washington and Abraham Lincoln, are combined into one celebration called President's Day, held on the third Monday of February.

George Washington, the first president of the United States, grew up on a large farm in Virginia in the 1700's. He learned how to plant vegetables, fruits, and grains. He used this knowledge as an adult when he designed his estate, Mount Vernon.

General George Washington was instrumental in winning the Revolutionary War against the British. He helped to define the new government and gave much of his life to public service.

Crab Cakes

Living near the Potomac River with seafood plentiful in that region, Washington loved to boat and fish. Here is a typical dish Washington might have eaten.

2 cups crab meat
1/4 cup milk
1/2 teaspoon dried parsley
1/4 cup dry bread crumbs
2 eggs, beaten
1 teaspoon Worcestershire sauce
2 tablespoons butter or margarine
2 tablespoons oil
Lemon wedges
Tartar sauce (see recipe below)

Tartar Sauce:
1/2 cup mayonnaise
1 tablespoon pickle relish <u>or</u>
  1 sweet pickle, finely diced

Children can stir together crabmeat, milk, parsley, bread crumbs, eggs, and Worcestershire sauce in a medium sized bowl.

Heat butter or margarine and oil in a large skillet over medium heat. Using a large spoon, adults need to drop the crab mixture into skillet to form 4 to 6 cakes. Sauté about 5 minutes on each side, or until brown. Serve on a bun or plain, with lemon and tartar sauce.

Yield: serves 4 to 6

Children can measure and mix mayonnaise and pickle together in a small bowl. Serve with crab cakes.

Yield: 1/2 cup

There is a myth about Washington in which he cut down a cherry tree when he was a boy. When his father asked, he said, "I cannot tell a lie. I chopped down the cherry tree." Whether the story is true or not, cherries have always been associated with Washington.

Washington Miniature Cherry Cheesecakes

These attractive cherry cheesecakes are quick, easy, and fun to make.

12 vanilla wafers
1 (8-oz.) cream cheese, softened
1/2 cup sugar
2 eggs
1 tablespoon lemon juice
1 teaspoon vanilla
One-half can of 21 oz. lite cherry pie filling
12 foil <u>or</u> paper baking cups

To soften cream cheese, leave out of refrigerator about an hour before preparing recipe, or microwave for 2 minutes on defrost power.

Preheat oven to 350 degrees F. Children can place paper-baking cups in muffin tin, and place one vanilla wafer in each, flat side up.

Beat cream cheese, sugar, eggs, lemon juice, and vanilla in a medium-sized bowl. Pour cream cheese mixture on top of vanilla wafer, filling about 3/4 full. (Don't worry if some vanilla wafers float. The cherries will cover and decorate the top.)

Bake for 15 minutes. Cool. Top with cherry pie filling. Refrigerate.

Yield: 12 miniature cheesecakes

Note: the remaining pie filling can be used to top pudding, pancakes, or ice cream parfaits.

America's sixteenth president, Abraham Lincoln, served during the Civil War between the North and South. He freed the slaves in 1863, and was assassinated two years later.

Author Janet Halliday Ervin says of Lincoln's eating habits in **The White House Cookbook**: *Deep in books or thoughts, he did not seem to care when nor what nor whether he ate. (He was probably the smallest eater of all the Presidents, being well satisfied with an apple or crackers and cheese in his office.)*

She quotes his law partner, Billy Herndon: *"Abe can sit and think longer without food than any man I ever met."* Other people remember he loved desserts, especially pecan pie. Perhaps his childhood, which was spent on the American frontier in the 1800's, prepared him for simple tastes in food, rather than an elaborate table of gourmet fare.

Old-Fashioned Buttermilk Biscuits

This bread recipe may have been one of the staples that Lincoln enjoyed in his log cabin home.

2 cups flour
1 tablespoon baking powder
1/2 teaspoon salt
1/3 cup shortening
1 cup buttermilk

Preheat oven to 450 degrees F.

Children can help measure and stir flour, baking powder, and salt in medium-sized bowl. Cut in shortening with a pastry blender or two knives until mixture looks like coarse meal. Add buttermilk; stir with a fork until just mixed.

Turn out dough onto a lightly floured cloth or board. Knead six times. Children will enjoy patting and shaping this dough. Give each child a bit of dough to play with. Use a floured rolling pin to roll dough ½ inch thick.

Cut with a 2-inch, floured biscuit cutter or drinking glass. Place on an ungreased cookie sheet, one-inch apart. Bake 12 minutes, or until lightly browned.

Yield: 12 biscuits

Yeasted Brown Raisin Bread

This may have been another Lincoln favorite.

3 cups rolled oats
1 tablespoon salt
2 tablespoons shortening
1 cup raisins
3 cups boiling water
1 package (2 1/2 teaspoons)
  active dry yeast
1 cup lukewarm water
1/2 cup honey
1/2 cup molasses
1 cup wheat bran
1 cup whole-wheat flour
7-8 cups white flour

Children can measure and combine rolled oats, salt, shortening, and raisins in a large bowl. An adult can pour boiling water over oat mixture and stir. Cool to lukewarm.

Test lukewarm water on your wrist, as for a baby bottle. It should feel warm, not hot. Children can dissolve yeast in lukewarm water; add to oat mixture along with honey, molasses, bran, and whole-wheat flour. Stir 100 times.

Add enough white flour to make a soft dough. Knead on a floured board or cloth 6 - 8 minutes. Add more flour to keep the dough from getting sticky. This fun activity is one kids can readily join in. Kneading is a systematic folding and turning of the dough to make it elastic and encourage yeast activity. Children can have fun punching, shaping, and playing with the dough as they knead.

Place dough in a greased bowl, turning to grease top. Cover with a clean towel and let rise in a draft-free place until double in bulk, about 1 1/2 hours.

Grease two 9 x 5-inch loaf pans. Mold dough into 2 loaves and place in pans. Let rise an additional 1 1/2 hours.

Bake in a 375 degrees F oven for 1 hour. Turn out of loaf pan to cool. Cool before slicing, if you can wait.

Yield: 2 loaves

St. Patrick's Day

On March 17, St. Patrick's Day, people from all backgrounds and cultures can claim to be a wee bit Irish. This is a day of parades and celebrations. It is a day to wear green. On this day rivers are dyed green, as are bagels and other foods.

St. Patrick is the patron saint of Ireland. He was a courageous missionary, who used the shamrock to illustrate the Christian trinity of God the Father, the Son, and Holy Spirit. The shamrock, or clover, is the symbol of St. Patrick's Day. He died on March 17, about 460 A.D.

Corned beef and cabbage is a traditional meal for St. Patrick's Day. Corned beef has been soaked in a brine, similar to pickles. Some children do not like cabbage or sauerkraut very well, but they might enjoy the beef and potatoes. Potatoes are a main part of many Irish meals. Serve corned beef and cabbage with Irish Soda Bread. Recipes follow for delicious dishes you can make with corned beef, such as Reuben Sandwiches and Corned Beef Hash.

Corned Beef, Cabbage, and Potatoes

3-pound corned beef brisket
6 potatoes
1 cabbage, cut into wedges

Children can help rinse corned beef with cold water to remove excess spices and salt. Place in a large pot and cover with water. Bring to a boil. Turn down heat and simmer, covered, until tender, about 3 hours.

Remove beef from pot and place on cutting board. Peel potatoes, and cut into fourths. Place potatoes and cabbage wedges in pot to cook with the broth. Bring to a boil, and then turn down heat and simmer, covered, for about fifteen minutes until vegetables are tender.

Meanwhile, carve the beef. Serve beef slices, potatoes, and cabbage on a platter.

Yield: 6 - 8 servings

Irish Soda Bread

4 cups flour
1 teaspoon baking soda
1 teaspoon salt
1 1/2 cups buttermilk

Preheat oven to 400 degrees F. Grease a cookie sheet.

Children can measure and stir together flour, baking soda, and salt in a large bowl. Make a well in the center and stir in buttermilk. Dough should form a ball.

On a floured board or cloth, children can knead and shape dough into a round loaf, about 8 inches across. Place dough in the center of the cookie sheet. Score bread dough with a sharp knife; make an X about 1/2-inch deep. Bake for about 40 minutes, until brown. Serve hot.

Yield: 1 loaf

Reuben Sandwiches

8 slices rye bread
Soft butter or margarine,
   about 3 tablespoons
4 slices corned beef
4 slices Swiss cheese
8 tablespoons sauerkraut (optional)

Heat a large skillet or griddle over medium heat. Children can spread butter or margarine on one side of bread. Make sandwich out of beef, cheese, and if they like it, sauerkraut. Keep the buttered side of the bread to the outside.

Place sandwiches in skillet. Grill just a few minutes, until brown, then turn over and grill until brown. Serve hot.

Yield: 4 sandwiches

Corned Beef Hash

2 tablespoon oil
2 cups chopped corned beef
3 cups chopped cooked potatoes
1 onion, chopped
Salt and pepper to taste

Heat oil in large skillet. Children can help chop beef, potatoes, and onions; add to skillet. Fry over medium heat until brown. Turn over and cook until brown. Add salt and pepper to taste. Good served with fried or poached eggs.

Yield: 4 servings

Variation for Red Flannel Hash: add 1 cup cooked diced beets to skillet when adding other ingredients.

SPRING IDEAS

- Plant at least one vegetable in a garden or clay pot.

- For April Fool's Day, tell your child a fib about what you are going to eat, then immediately say "April Fool!"

- For May Day bring a bunch of flowers, and a basket of fresh-baked muffins to a neighbor's doorstep. Knock and run away.

- For Easter, color and hide eggs with your child.

- For Mother's Day, discuss what foods are mom's favorite and grandma's favorite.

- For Father's Day, discuss what foods are dad's favorite and grandpa's favorite.

Teaching Children Hope

Spring is a time for hope. It is a time to rejoice in new life after the winter. You can teach your child hope, and what better time than during this season?

Remember the story of **The Engine That Could**? The little blue engine puffed, "*I think I can, I think I can...*" when trying to pull toys and food to boys and girls over the mountain? This little train was willing to take on this task and achieved his goal because he had hope. He puffed steadily down the mountain: "*I thought I could; I thought I could.*"

Dr. Charles R. Snyder, a psychologist at the University of Kansas who studies hope, defines hope as more than the simple notion that everything will turn out all right. "*Having hope means believing you have both the will and the way to accomplish your goals, whatever they may be.*"

Should We Teach Hope?

In the world we live in today, with crime, violence, and war, you may wonder if it is healthy to teach children to hope. You might reason it is better to be realistic and teach children that ours is a cold, cruel world without hope. If you teach children to hope, is it just setting them up for disappointment when they grow to adulthood? The answer is NO!

Research shows that when a person, young or old, is hopeful, they are healthier, happier, and have better relationships with family, friends, and their community. Children have more chance to be successful in school. Grownups have more chance for better paying jobs and rewarding careers. If you teach your child to hope, he might not have better circumstances than another child, but he will be able to thrive with whatever challenges he faces.

Dr. Snyder's research included discovering what attributes hopeful people have, so we can learn how to be more like them.

> **Hopeful People:**
> - turn to friends to help achieve their goals
> - believe they can achieve their goals
> - tell themselves things get better with time
> - are flexible in finding ways to achieve a goal
> - take small steps to get to a goal
> - aim for another, possibly similar goal,
>   if they find they cannot achieve a desired goal

Goals are achieved by grownups as well as children. And children's goals are not that different from adult goals. Both children and adults hope for friendship with a peer, either a school classmate or co-worker. Both children and adults hope for someone to snuggle with: a teddy bear or a spouse. Both hope to master a sport: learning to jump rope, or learning to ski. Goals and hopes of any age need to be taken seriously.

As a parent or caregiver, you are the one who is most capable of helping your child embrace the attributes of hopeful people. You can be the friend to help her with a goal. You can tell her, "You can do it!" You can remind her she is growing and when she is a little older she will be able to reach her goal, for example, of jumping rope. By taking small steps you can help her learn. Maybe you'll point out she could jump over the rope, if you lay it flat on the ground. And take the next step of swinging it gently back and forth, low to the ground, while she jumps. If it's not the right time to achieve this goal, you could help with another, similar goal, such as hopping on one foot, walking backwards, skipping, etc. Whatever the goal, you can help your child by actively using the attributes of hopeful people.

One important point to remember is: a hopeful attitude is not a sit-back-and-wait attitude. Hope embraces motivation. When a child says, "I hope grandma visits us this spring," he has already begun the process of hope. He is going to find a way to accomplish this goal. There are several different approaches he can take: telling you is one, because you are the number one person who helps make this happen. He could continue to finalize his goal by writing a letter, e-mailing, or telephoning her. If his grandma is able to come, and she can afford it, such as the expense of a plane ticket, his hope will be realized.

All hope can be related to how we view our whole lives. Springtime is time to renew our hope and inspire that hope in our children. Now is the time to begin.

Hot Cross Buns

The symbol for Easter is the cross. This is an easy recipe for a traditional bread.

1 can refrigerated biscuits

Vanilla frosting in a squeezable tube

Children can place biscuits on a cookie sheet. Bake according to package directions. Let biscuits cool slightly. Squeeze the frosting in a cross pattern on each biscuit. Serve right away.

Yield: 10 buns

The egg is a symbol of birth and new life. The bunny rabbit is another symbol of spring. Following are recipes appropriate for this season.

Bunny's Favorite Egg Salad

This is the perfect way to use up Easter eggs!

4 eggs
1/4 cup mayonnaise
1 stalk celery, diced
1 tablespoon minced white onion
Salt and pepper

Cook eggs by placing them single layer in a small saucepan. Add enough cold water to cover eggs. Partially cover and bring to a rolling boil. Remove from heat and fully cover. Let eggs stand in hot water for 18-20 minutes to hard cook eggs. Pour off hot water and run cold water over eggs. Refrigerate until thoroughly cooled.

Children can peel eggs by cracking them on a paper towel. Rinse eggs under cool water. Place on a cutting board.

Children can help chop eggs with a butter knife, then place in a medium-sized mixing bowl. Mix in mayonnaise, celery, and onion. Add salt and pepper, if desired. Use on sandwiches, with crackers, or serve on a bed of lettuce.

Yield: 4 servings

Carrot Raisin Salad

Who likes carrots better than bunnies?

4 large carrots
1/4 cup mayonnaise or
* salad dressing*
2 tablespoons raisins
1 tablespoon sugar (optional)

Rinse and pare carrots. Grate into a medium-sized bowl. Children can help measure and add mayonnaise, raisins, and sugar. Stir to moisten.

Yield: 4 servings.

Bunny Salad

1 can pear halves
Raisins
Red cherries, candied or maraschino
Shredded cheese
Marshmallows
Lettuce

Drain juice from pears. Wash lettuce and put a lettuce leaf on individual plate.

To make bunny:
Place pear halve face down on lettuce leaf.
Put 2 raisins on the pear for the eyes.
Use a red cherry for the nose.
Put several pieces of shredded cheese on each side of face for whiskers.
Cut two marshmallows in half and use for ears of bunny.
Add a marshmallow for the bunny's tail.

Bunny's Favorite Sandwiches

Green onion, sliced
Soft cream cheese
Pumpernickel bread

Mix green onion with cream cheese. Children can spread cream cheese mixture on one slice bread and place another piece of bread on top. Cut into fourths and serve on pretty platter.

Spring Flowers Cake

Use any prepared cake mix that color coordinates with any spring flowers available, such as tulips or daffodils. Bake the cake in a bundt pan. When the cake comes out of the oven, transfer to a cooling rack for 15 minutes. Then, an adult can turn the serving plate upside down over the cake pan and turn the cake over onto the plate. Pull the pan up off the cake. Let the cake cool; to serve, either dust with powdered sugar or serve plain.

Children can place a bunch of spring flowers that have the stems wrapped in aluminum foil in the center of the cake (the hole in the center). Now you have a beautiful spring-time centerpiece and dessert combined in one!

Just Foolin'

Why not encourage the spirit of April Fool's Day, April 1, by having fun at mealtimes? When my daughter was seven years old, she reminded me of the year before, when I put juice in the cereal bowls and breakfast cereal in the juice glasses on April Fool's Day. "Can you do that again, Mommy?" she pleaded.

Tricks are funny even when they are not a surprise, and sometimes even more, because we can anticipate what will happen. There are appropriate times and ways to "play" at mealtimes. Can you think of some April Fool's tricks on your own? Your child is sure to catch on! Be sure to explain you are "just fooling!" Here are some ideas:

• *Switching containers.* If you usually serve juice in a cup, try a mug, or a bowl. Breakfast cereal can be placed in a cup or pan. If you serve cereal on a plate, your child might ask, "What will happen when I pour on the milk?" Don't limit your tricks to breakfast. How about a sandwich served on a cutting board or a sliced apple in a salad bowl?

• *Switching order.* Do you ever have three course meals? Do you serve the salad first, then the main dish and finish with dessert? What kind of look would your child give you if you served dessert first? Then continue your meal with the main dish and end with salad. If you try this one, let's hope you and your child have room for the main meal.

• *Hide & Seek.* When you're serving spaghetti or another dish with sauce, hide the sauce by serving it first on the plate, then place the spaghetti on top. Some fine restaurants serve the sauce first for a dish such a veal Parmesan. This way, the breaded veal cutlet doesn't get soggy. You can hide syrup under pancakes, cheese under crackers, butter under bread...

• *Switch Utensils.* Try eating soup with a fork, or salad with bread sticks, or rice with your fingers. How silly! Try eating a hamburger with a spoon, cereal with a fork, and spaghetti with your fingers. Be sure to explain to your child that you are only trying this out and this is not the norm. Every once and a while you might want to do it again, or you could just reserve April as the month for fun ways to eat.

• *Upside down.* When you set the table, set it with the cups and plates upside down. Have your child help you "set it right" before serving.

• *Switch places.* Do you have a certain place to sit? We do. One day you could sit where your child usually sits, or use different chairs. If you have a dining room, eat there for no special reason.

April 1st can be full of surprises not only in the way you eat, but what you serve. This meat loaf tastes delicious, looks pretty, and is economical. Serve with Surprise Baked Potatoes and Surprise Biscuits. Add the "no-surprise" Spinach Power squares and you have an oven meal that will get rave reviews. Some fresh carrot sticks or other veggies will make a nice addition to your menu.

Surprise Meat Loaf

Here is a recipe from my grandmother. The surprise is the hard cooked eggs in the center.

3 eggs (2 to hard-cook,
  1 to mix in with ground beef)
1/2 onion
1/4 cup bread crumbs
1/2 teaspoon salt
1 pound ground beef

Hard cook 2 eggs (see page 75, **Bunny's Favorite Egg Salad** for method of hard cooking eggs). When eggs are cool enough to handle, children can help peel them. Set aside.

As you and your child crack the 1 remaining (uncooked) egg into a large bowl, point out the difference between uncooked and hard-cooked eggs. Use a cheese grater to grate onion and add to bowl, along with bread crumbs, salt, and ground beef. Mix thoroughly.

Pack about a third of the meat mixture into an 8 x 4-inch loaf pan; place hard-cooked eggs on top, then surround hard-cooked eggs with the remaining meat mixture. Bake in 350 degree F oven for 1 hour. Slice and serve hot. When you slice the loaf, a circle of hard-cooked eggs should be in each slice.

Yield: 4 servings

Surprise Baked Potatoes

4 baking potatoes
Butter
Salt and pepper
Milk
4 teaspoons bacon bits
Grated Cheddar cheese

Bake potatoes in oven with meat loaf for 1 hour. Slice in half and scoop out potato into a bowl; set aside potato peel. (Potato will be hot.) Children can mash potato with butter, salt and pepper to taste, and add enough milk to make mixture fluffy.

Pile potato back into skins. Poke bacon bits into center. Top with grated cheddar cheese, and bake for 15 minutes, or until hot and cheese is melted.

Yield: 4 - 8 servings

Surprise Biscuits

1 can refrigerated biscuits,
   10 count
Ten 1/2 inch cubes of Cheddar
   cheese

Preheat oven according to package directions, about 400 degrees F. Let child place a cheese cube in the center of each biscuit. Then let him roll the dough into a ball to enclose the cheese cube inside the biscuit dough. (You can model this action first.)

Place on cookie sheet, with the seam face up, so that when the biscuit bakes, the cheese will not run out, but melt inside. Bake according to package directions, about 10 minutes.

Yield: 10 biscuits

Spinach Power

2 packages (10 oz. each) frozen
   chopped spinach, thawed
4 tablespoons butter or margarine
3 eggs
1 cup unbleached flour
1 teaspoon baking powder
2 teaspoons salt
Pepper to taste
1 cup milk
10 oz. Monterey Jack cheese, grated
1 onion, cut up

Drain spinach. Children can help drain the spinach through a strainer and squeeze dry with paper towel.

Melt butter in the oven in a 13 x 9-inch pan.

Children can use rotary hand egg beater and beat eggs in large mixing bowl.

Stir in flour, baking powder, and seasonings. Gradually stir in milk. Mix well. Add spinach, cheese, and onion. Mix until well blended.

Pour into pan with the melted butter or margarine. Bake in 350 degree F oven for 35 minutes.

Cut into squares for serving. Serve hot.

Yield: 24 squares

Here are other recipes to try for more surprises!

Dirt Pile Pudding

1 large (5 oz.) package chocolate instant pudding, prepared with skim milk
1 cup whipped topping
1 cup chocolate cookie crumbs
Gummy worms

Children can help prepare pudding according to package directions, using skim milk. Fold in whipped topping.

Spoon dessert into individual dishes and hide a gummy worm half way into the pudding.

To make cookie crumbs, place cookies in plastic or paper sack and crush with rolling pin.

Top pudding with cookie crumbs.

Yield: 12 1/2-cup servings

Little Topper Cakes

Cake mix, any flavor
1 (1 oz.) package pudding mix, either instant or cooked variety
Powdered sugar

Grease muffin pans for 24 cupcakes. Children can help prepare cake mix according to directions. Pour prepared batter into muffin pans, filling one-half full. Bake as directed on package. Cool.

Meanwhile, prepare pudding mix according to package directions. If using the cooked pudding, make sure to cool before proceeding.

When cupcakes have cooled, cut a deep circle out of the top of each cupcake. Pour pudding into center of each cupcake. Carefully replace the top of cupcake. Dust cupcakes with powdered sugar. Serve.

Yield: 24 cupcakes

May Day

The first day of May is a celebration of flowers. As the rhyme goes, "April showers bring May flowers." May day activities center around these beautiful signs of spring.

Two traditional activities are perfect for children. The first is to set a basket of flowers on a friend's doorstep, knock on the door and run away. Flowers need not be expensive. They can be grown in your garden, and can include "wild," silk, or even paper flowers. Children love the running away!

The second activity is dancing around a May pole, which has colorful ribbons connected to the top. By holding the end of each ribbon, the colors are woven back and forth until the pole is covered. (Poles do not need to be full size.)

Besides flowers, the month of May signals spring fruits, such as strawberries, which are in season.

Strawberry Parfait

1 pint fresh strawberries
One of the following:
  2 cups vanilla pudding
  1 pint vanilla ice cream
  12-oz. cottage cheese
  16-oz. yogurt
1/4 cup granola

These look prettiest in parfait glasses, which are tall, clear glass dessert dishes. Then the layers of red and white are clearly visible.

Children can pull or trim the stems from the strawberries. Rinse, and then slice in half with a butter knife.

Children can place a layer of strawberries in the dessert dish. Top with pudding, ice cream, cottage cheese, or yogurt. Repeat until you reach the top of the parfait glass or until you have a single serving. Each dessert is layered in a separate glass or bowl.

Top with a sprinkling of granola. Serve or chill until serving time.

Yield: 4 - 6 parfaits

Individual Strawberry Shortcakes

1 quart fresh strawberries
1/2 to 3/4 cup sugar
2 cups flour
2 tablespoons sugar
1 tablespoon baking powder
1 teaspoon salt
1/3 cup shortening
3/4 cup milk
About 3 tablespoons softened
  butter
Whipped cream

Children can rinse and hull strawberries; slice. Sprinkle with 1/2 to 3/4 cup sugar. Cover and set in refrigerator. The sugar and berries will turn into a wonderful strawberry-syrup in about an hour.

Measure flour, 2 tablespoons sugar, baking powder, and salt into medium-sized bowl. Cut in shortening with pastry blender or 2 knives. Stir in milk. Turn out onto floured board or cloth.

Children can knead dough lightly 20 times. Then roll dough 1/2-inch thick with rolling pin. Cut with biscuit cutter or glass into eight 2 1/2-inch circles. Place on ungreased cookie sheet. Bake in 450 degrees F oven for 10 - 12 minutes or until golden brown.

To serve: split shortcake in half; spread with soft butter (about a teaspoon per shortcake). Top with strawberry mixture and whipped cream.

Yield: 8 servings

Fresh Fruit Kabobs

1 small can (8 oz.) pineapple chunks
2 bananas
12 fresh strawberries
18 seedless grapes
Wooden skewers

Drain pineapple chunks, saving the juice in a small bowl. Peel bananas and cut each into 6 pieces. Children can use a butter knife to cut bananas. Place bananas in the pineapple juice to help prevent browning. Wash and remove the stems of strawberries with a teaspoon. Wash the grapes.

On each skewer, place a pineapple chunk, banana chunk, grape, and strawberry, ending up with two or three of each on a skewer.

Yield: 6 servings

Fruity Smoothie

Frosty, creamy, light, and healthy

1 cup fresh <u>or</u> frozen strawberries
1 frozen banana, cut in chunks
2 cups orange juice
1/2 cup instant nonfat dry
   milk powder
2 teaspoons honey

Children can help prepare fruit and measure ingredients. Place all the ingredients in blender. Blend until smooth.

Yield: 2 servings

No-Sugar Strawberry Freezer Jam

4 cups fresh strawberries,
   stemmed and halved
1 1/2 cup white grape juice
2 1/2 tablespoon lemon juice
1/4 teaspoon grated lemon rind
Dash salt
2 envelopes unflavored gelatin

First, prepare fruit. Children can pull the green stems off the berries and use a butter or dinner knife to cut the strawberries in half. Place the grape juice in a 4 quart saucepan and bring to a boil. Boil down to 1/2 cup juice. *Watch carefully so it doesn't burn.*

Remove from heat; add strawberries, lemon juice, rind, and salt to pot. *Be careful, as the mixture is very hot!*

Mash with potato masher to release strawberry juice, then heat to boiling. Sprinkle gelatin over hot mixture, stirring well to dissolve. Remove from heat. Cool and pour into plastic containers for freezing. Leave space in containers for expansion.

Yield: 4 cups (4 half-pint jars)

Spinach Salad

Fresh, tender spinach, mixed with other vegetables or even fruit, is tasty and healthy. Unwashed spinach will keep in the refrigerator for four or five days. Wash just before using, as wet spinach tends to spoil quickly and its leaves will bruise more easily.

Fresh spinach, bunch
2 kiwi
1/4 small onion, cut in rings

Dressing:
1/2 cup sugar
1/2 cup water
1/2 teaspoon dry mustard
2 tablespoons vinegar
1 egg, beaten

Children can help wash and dry spinach and tear into bowl, removing and discarding stem. Adult may need to peel kiwi and cut onion rings. Divide spinach into individual salad bowls. Top with sliced kiwi. Sprinkle onion rings over the top.

Children can measure sugar, water, mustard, and vinegar into a small saucepan. Adults will need to stir and heat dressing until it boils and becomes slightly thickened.

Remove from heat and slowly add to 1 beaten egg. Pour back into pan, replace on heat, and bring just to a boil. Serve hot or cold over salad.

Yield: Serves 4-6

Crunchy Chicken Salad

1 cup cut-up chicken
 (can use canned)
1 cup chopped celery
1 cup grated carrots
1/2 cup cut-up onion
1/2 cup mayonnaise
1 (1 .7 oz.) can shoestring
 potatoes
Lettuce

Children can help with chopping celery, grating carrots, and perhaps cutting up the onion. Mix vegetables with chicken and mayonnaise.

Just before serving, mix in the shoestring potatoes. Serve on lettuce leaf.

Yield: 4 servings

Cinco de Mayo
A Mexican Fiesta

Cinco de Mayo, May 5, is the day Mexican people remember the victory of a battle over French ruler Napoleon III's army in 1862. It is a day of feasting and celebration.

Mexican food is colorful, spicy, and a perfect choice for a "fiesta." The word "fiesta" means "a festival, or church-feast holiday." A "fiesta" is thought of as a "party." And the best parties include good food.

One reason children like Mexican food is that many foods are finger foods, ones that we pick up with our hands. Of course, there is also the delicious, spicy flavor and the blend of textures that make Mexican food so popular.

Foods common to Mexican cooking are: chili peppers, either mild or spicy; beans, red, black, or pinto; tortillas, a pancake-like bread made of cornmeal or flour; and fresh fruits and vegetables, such as tomatoes, limes, and avocados.

Some of the snacks in Mexico have become meals in the United States. This is true of the taco, which are sold by street vendors South-of-the-Border as a between meal snack. However, Mexican food is much more than the tacos and burritos we know. Based on the food of the Aztec Indians and European Spaniards, Mexican food is varied and delicious.

Add excitement to your fiesta by using a brightly colored tablecloth, a candle centerpiece, and any native Mexican artifacts you might have, such as their beautifully crafted pottery. Purchase or create a piñata, a paper maché form, usually the shape of an animal, filled with treats.

Which of the following recipes will become a family favorite?

Avocado Dip

2 ripe avocados
2 tablespoons lemon juice
2 mild green chilies, minced
1/4 teaspoon salt
Tortilla chips

Cut avocados in half. Remove pits and show children how large the pits are in comparison to the fruit. Scoop pulp into a bowl. Discard rind. Children can mash avocado pulp with a fork or potato masher. Stir in lemon juice, chilies, and salt. Serve with tortilla chips.

Yield: about 1 1/2 cups.

To grow avocado pit: suspend with toothpicks in a jar of water. Set on a sunny windowsill.

Skinny Nachos

1 (14-oz.) package baked tortilla
   chips
1 (8-oz.) package low-fat, shredded
   Cheddar cheese
1 (4-oz.) can of mild green chilies

Place a layer of tortilla chips on a microwaveable plate. Children can sprinkle chips with a liberal amount of shredded cheese. Top with chopped chilies. Microwave for 45 seconds on high; serve.

Note: can be made in a conventional oven: bake on a cookie sheet at 400 degrees F. for 5 minutes.

Soft Taco

1 pound ground beef
1 onion, chopped
1 teaspoon chili powder
1 tablespoon flour
1/2 cup water
1 tomato, diced
1/4 head lettuce, shredded
1 cup grated low-fat Cheddar cheese
1 package (10) whole wheat
   flour tortillas
Mild bottled salsa, about 8-oz.

Brown ground beef and onion in large skillet over medium heat. Drain grease, if necessary. Stir in chili powder and flour, and then add water. Turn down heat, cover, and simmer a few minutes to blend flavors.

Children can help dice tomato, shred lettuce, and grate cheese.

Heat flour tortillas in non-stick skillet, conventional oven, or microwave until warm. Serve family style, with bowls of beef mixture, tomatoes, lettuce, cheese, and salsa. Fill tortillas. Fold over and serve warm.

Yield: 4 servings

Poke-a-Dot Rice

2 tablespoons oil
1 1/2 cups brown rice
1 clove garlic, minced
1 onion, diced
1 red pepper, diced
3 cups chicken stock <u>or</u> bouillon

Children can help measure and prepare ingredients first. Heat oil in a 3-quart saucepan. Add rice, garlic, onion, and pepper. Stir occasionally over medium heat until rice is golden brown, about 10 minutes. Take off heat, let cool slightly. Then add stock slowly and carefully, as it will splatter. Place on heat and bring to a boil. Turn down heat to low and cover.

Simmer for 1 hour, or until all liquid is absorbed. Serve hot.

Yield: 4 servings

Fajitas

Beef _or_ chicken, uncooked, boneless
Marinade
Olive oil
Red pepper
Green pepper
Onion
Refried beans
Tomatoes
Ripe olives
Lettuce
Soft shell tortillas
Grated cheese
Sour cream

Adults will need to cut up uncooked beef or chicken in small strips. Place in bowl and pour marinade over meat. This can be store-bought marinade, your own, or use Italian salad dressing. Cover bowl and refrigerate at least two hours.

Cut peppers and onions into thin slices and sauté in olive oil in frying pan. Remove to bowl and brown meat in same pan until tender. Add refried beans. Heat.

Children can help chop fresh tomatoes and olives. Shred lettuce.

Wrap tortillas in foil and heat in oven or warm in microwave by placing each on microwaveable plate with paper towel between and on top of tortilla.

Spoon beef or chicken, sautéed vegetables, and rest of ingredients into warmed tortillas. Roll up.

Yield: 1 pound meat serves 4

Tortilla Wraps

1 (8 oz.) cream cheese
1 (8-oz.) carton sour cream
Green onions, chopped
Ripe olives, chopped
1 cup grated Cheddar cheese
Large flour tortillas
1 jar Picante sauce

Soften cream cheese. Children can mix in sour cream.

Chop green onions and olives. Add green onions, olives, and cheese to cream cheese mixture. Spread over flour tortillas.

Roll up, cover, and refrigerate at least 2 hours. To serve, slice each roll into 8 - 10 slices.

Serve with Picante sauce.

Yield: about 6 large tortilla rolls

Tortilla Snacks

Small corn tortillas
Grated cheese
Salsa or Picante sauce
Sour cream

Place tortillas in frying pan over medium heat, or use electric fry pan. Heat for 1 to 2 minutes and turn over.

Cover tortillas with grated cheese. Top each with another tortilla and turn over. Heat for a few minutes until warmed and cheese is melted.

Remove from pan and cut in half or quarters. Serve with salsa or Picante sauce and sour cream.

Other ingredients can be added to cheese, such as ham, chicken, mushrooms, olives, etc.

Cinnamon-Chocolate Pudding with Meringue

2 cups prepared chocolate pudding,
  homemade, store bought or a mix
1/2 teaspoon cinnamon
2 egg whites
1/4 cup sugar

Preheat oven to 400 degrees F.

Place chocolate pudding in a 1-quart casserole. Children can mix cinnamon with pudding.

Beat egg whites on highest speed of electric mixer until soft peaks form. Add sugar, one tablespoon at a time, beating until stiff peaks form.

Spread meringue to the edges of the pudding. Bake for 5 to 6 minutes, or until golden brown. Serve warm or cold.

Yield: 4 servings

Mother's Day
Dad and Kids Cook to Surprise Mom

It was 7 a.m. Mother's Day morning. I dozed back to sleep and awoke to the pleasant sounds from the kitchen, muffled by the closed bedroom door. Water was running; utensils were clanking; the coffee was brewing. And the aroma! Was it pancakes? I heard the deep voice of my husband directing my daughter as they prepared breakfast.

Want to surprise your wife, and show her how much you love her? Let her sleep late on Mother's Day, while you and the kids get up and cook breakfast. After a hectic weekday schedule, she will appreciate the TLC (tender loving care) and you will be able to spend some time with your kids.

Guidelines for Dads

- Find an unhurried time
- Start with a simple recipe.
- Choose a short recipe.
- Choose a recipe you have made before by yourself.
- Keep safety in mind.
- Allow children to participate away from heat and sharp utensils.
- Relax about messes and spills.
- Get the kids involved in cooking, serving, and clean up.

Cooking = Learning

Cooking time is structured play activity, where kids are not there just to "help out", but to learn math concepts, such as measuring, and social skills, such as cooperation.

You can use dramatic play while cooking. For example, you could say, *"I'm Chef Boyardee, and you are my two assistants."* This helps keep children on task. Maybe your child would not want to clean up a spill, but an official Chef Boyardee assistant would!

What memories do you have about your dad cooking? Mine often made pancakes. One friend of mine has wonderful childhood memories of watching her dad make candy during the winter holidays. Some dads might be the director while cooking. Other dads might prefer to be a participator. Whatever your role, encourage your child to help by giving clear, specific directions.

Start with Breakfast

When asking dads about cooking, breakfast on the weekend was the favorite meal to cook. This is an unhurried time when many families can change from the cereal and milk menu and plan a bigger breakfast, or a cooked breakfast.

During the preparation time, dads and kids can catch up on their weekdays' happenings and feelings. Adults and children may find it easier to talk while they are cooking, rather than sitting down just to talk. Talking and reflecting about the past week can get everyone ready to face a new week.

Below are recipes to try with your child on Mother's Day, the second Sunday in May.

Multi-Grain Pancakes

1 1/2 cups white flour
1/4 cup whole wheat flour
2 tablespoons wheat germ
4 teaspoons baking powder
1/2 teaspoon salt
2 eggs, lightly beaten
1 3/4 cups milk
1/4 cup melted butter

Preheat griddle on medium-high (400 degrees F) while mixing batter. Children can measure dry ingredients into a medium-sized bowl. Make a well in the center and add eggs, milk, and butter or margarine. Stir with a wooden spoon until large lumps disappear. (Small lumps are OK.) Pour about 1 tablespoon oil onto griddle and spread with a pancake turner.

Note: The griddle gets very hot. Older children might be able to ladle batter onto griddle.

Ladle batter onto griddle in approximately 4-inch circles. When the edges are cooked, but before bubbles pop, turn pancakes. Cook briefly on flip side. Keep pancakes on a platter, covered with a cloth towel to keep warm, until all batter is cooked.

Low fat pancake toppings
· fresh fruit
· fruited yogurt
· cottage cheese

Serve with your favorite filling or topping (see following recipes).

Yield: about 1 dozen pancakes

To Mom on Mother's Day —

Serve breakfast to Mom on a tray, with fresh fruit, a cloth napkin, a flower, and a Mother's Day card. She'll know how much you appreciate her!

Pigs in a Blanket

Cook link sausage. Wrap each sausage in a pancake.

Boiled Maple Syrup

1 cup light corn syrup
1/2 cup brown sugar
1/2 cup water
1/4 teaspoon maple extract

Children can measure corn syrup, brown sugar, and water into a 1-quart saucepan. Adults should bring this to a boil while stirring, to prevent sugar from burning. Then turn down heat to low and simmer 5 minutes. Remove from heat and add maple extract. Serve over pancakes or waffles.

Note: syrup gets very hot. Caution!

Cinnamon Apple Syrup

4 cooking apples, pared, cored, and sliced
1 cup water
1/2 cup sugar
1 tablespoon cornstarch
1/2 teaspoon cinnamon
1/4 teaspoon nutmeg

Prepare apples. Children can mix all ingredients in a medium-sized saucepan. Place on stove but adults need to watch this, as it gets very hot. Bring to a boil. Turn down heat to low and simmer, covered, for 15 minutes, or until apples are soft.

Serve on pancakes, waffles, plain cake or ice cream.

Mother's Day Luncheon

Instead of a breakfast, surprise Mom with a colorful luncheon—one that will be sure to please her. Add a tossed green garden salad and a croissant to the following casserole main dish and Mom will be dazzled with your planning and cooking ingenuity.

Chicken Casserole

2 3/4 cups chicken, cooked and
   diced
2 cups small shell macaroni,
   uncooked
1 (10.5 oz.) can cream of chicken
   soup
1 (10.5 oz.) can mushroom soup
1 soup can milk
1 (13.5 oz.) can chicken broth
1 small onion, chopped
1 (5 oz.) can water chestnuts, sliced
1 (8 oz.) grated cheddar cheese

Add cooked and diced chicken to large bowl. Children can measure and add macaroni, soups, milk, and chicken broth. Add chopped onion, sliced water chestnuts, and half of the cheese.

Spoon mixture into greased 13 x 9-inch baking pan. Top with remainder of grated cheddar cheese. Bake casserole at 350 degrees F for 1 hour or until it is golden brown and bubbling in the center.

Yield: 6 - 8 servings

Strawberry Slush

1 1/2 cups fresh strawberries
1 cup milk
2 teaspoons sugar (optional)

Children can rinse, hull and prick each strawberry with a fork. Place in a container; cover and freeze until firm.

Place all ingredients in blender. Blend for about 10 seconds. Pour into a glass and drink.

Yield: 2 - 4 servings

Father's Day
Invitations to a Brunch

Father's Day, the third Sunday in June, is a special day when we honor our fathers. It's the perfect time for family or friends to get-together for a brunch, which is a mid-morning meal that serves both as breakfast and lunch.

Although the telephone might be a quicker way to invite others to join in the meal, making your own invitations is more fun. You and your child can plan, create, and send invitations, and look forward to the big day!

Once you make invitations together, the basics apply to other events such as birthdays and holiday parties. Invitations help to clarify the reason for the get-together, and serve as reminders of who is hosting the event, where it is held, and when they should arrive.

What to Include

Whether you make your own invitations, or buy them ready to fill out, specific information should be included, such as:

Name: (Whose brunch)
Address: (Where the brunch will take place)
Date: (Day of the week, month and date)
Time: (Beginning and ending times)
Phone Number: (Home number, with best time to call)
R.S.V.P.: (Explain to your child this is a French saying that means, "respond or call back, if you please." Then you will know how many people can come.)

Creating Your Own Invitations

It is relatively easy for you and your child to create your own invitations on the computer, or by hand. You will need paper, crayons or magic markers, envelopes, and stamps.
Your child can:
• decide what color paper to use
• draw a picture on the paper
• sign a scribble for his name, a letter in her name or the full name
• put completed invitation in the envelope
• apply the stamp

Depending on your child's age, an adult may need to:
- decide how many people to invite
- write the information on each invitation
- address the envelopes

Telephone Etiquette

Before a parent calls to R.S.V.P., talk to your child about what to say. For young children, keep it simple. For example, when you answer the phone say, "Hello". Find out who is calling. Let an adult have a turn on the phone to clarify information. Say "good-bye" before hanging up.

For older children, explain about the impression they make on whoever is calling. Being polite is of the utmost importance. Whether your telephone calls are from family or friends, or for business purposes, everyone appreciates good telephone etiquette.

Explain to your child that 90% of communication is conveyed through "body language." When we cannot see each other, our words and the tone of our voice are the only way we have to communicate. So words become more important on the telephone than when we see each other face to face.

Enunciation is important, too. Tell children to say "yes" instead of "yeah." Keep a pad of paper and pen by each telephone to write a note during or after the conversation if a phone number or message needs to be reported to another person.

The Day Before

With the planning, involvement, and anticipation, the brunch will be twice as special, for your kids, their father, or grandfather! Here are some recipes to make for your Father's Day Brunch. The cake can be baked and frozen beforehand, if desired. The egg casserole should be made the day before, refrigerated overnight, and baked the morning of the brunch. Muffins can be made the day before, in fact, their flavor increases overnight; warm them up before the meal. The salad should be mixed with the cheese and sour cream just before serving.

Fresh Fruit Cup

1 cup strawberries, stemmed and
  rinsed
1 cup cherries, stemmed and pitted
1 cup green grapes, cut in half
1 cup sliced peaches
1 cup melon balls
2 bananas, peeled and sliced
Orange juice

Children can help prepare fruit. Place in large bowl. Pour just enough orange juice over fruit mixture to moisten.

Spoon into attractive dishes and serve.

 Yield: 8 servings

Good Morning Muffins

3/4 cup sugar
1 cup flour
2 teaspoons baking powder
1/2 teaspoon baking soda
1/4 teaspoon salt
2 teaspoons cinnamon
1 cup crushed pineapple, drained
1/2 cup raisins
1/2 cup coconut
1/2 cup nuts, chopped
3 eggs
3/4 cup vegetable oil
2 cups carrots, finely chopped <u>or</u>
   2 cups junior baby food carrots
2 teaspoons vanilla

Children can help combine dry ingredients in large mixing bowl. They can stir in drained pineapple, raisins, coconut, and nuts.

 Make a hole in center of dry ingredients and add eggs, oil, carrots, and vanilla. Stir only until ingredients are moistened.

Grease 24 muffin cups, or use paper liners, and fill 2/3 full.

Bake in 350 degrees F oven for 20 - 25 minutes or until muffins are lightly brown and spring back when touched. Cool for 5 minutes and remove to rack to finish cooling.

These can be made the day before (their flavor develops by setting overnight) and warmed in aluminum foil in the oven before serving.

Yield: 24 muffins

Cheesy Egg Casserole

1 pound ham, cubed
8 slices American cheese
8 slices bread, cubed
6 eggs
2 1/4 cups milk
1 1/4 teaspoon dry mustard

Grease 13 x 9-inch pan. Reserve 1/2 cup of bread cubes. Children can place remaining bread cubes in pan, then ham cubes, and top with cheese slices.

In a large bowl, beat eggs, milk, and dry mustard. Pour in pan over all. Top with 1/2 cup bread cubes. Cover with plastic wrap and refrigerate overnight.

The next day, remove plastic wrap and bake 1 hour at 350 degrees F. Cut into squares. Serve hot.

Yield: 8 - 10 servings

Country Salad

1/2 pound fresh spinach
1 bunch romaine lettuce
1 head lettuce
2 tomatoes
1 red onion
1 cucumber
2 carrots
1 cup sour cream
1 cup cottage cheese
Salt and pepper to taste

Have a large bowl for the salad. Add each ingredient to the bowl after preparing. Children can help wash and dry the greens.

To wash spinach: place in a bowl of cold water. Swish. Sand will fall to the bottom of the bowl. Remove spinach from bowl by handfuls; place in colander to drain, and pat dry with clean towel. Remove stems and tear into bite-size pieces. Rinse, drain, and pat lettuce dry. Tear into small pieces.

Cut each tomato into 8 wedges. Slice onion in thin rings. Pare and slice cucumber. Pare and shred carrots. Chill salad.

Before serving, toss salad with a dressing of sour cream, cottage cheese, and salt and pepper to taste.

Yield: 10 servings

Brunch Cake

1 1/2 cups flour
1 cup sugar
1/2 cup butter
2 teaspoons baking powder
1 egg
1 teaspoon vanilla
1/2 cup milk
1/2 cup raisins
1/2 cup diced apple

Grease and flour an 8 or 9-inch square pan. Preheat oven to 350 degrees F.

Blend flour, sugar, and butter with a pastry blender or two knives until butter is the size of small peas. Reserve 1/2 cup of this crumb mixture for topping.

Children can add remaining ingredients and stir just until mixed. Pour into pan. Sprinkle on topping. Bake about 50-55 minutes or until golden.

Yield: 9 - 12 servings

Homemade Hot Cocoa Mix

Make some hot cocoa for children and hot mocha for parents. Mocha Mix, which combines the taste of chocolate and coffee, would be a perfect gift to give each father that attends. Just place mix in a jar, tie with a ribbon, and include directions.

1 (26-oz.) box non-fat dry milk
1 (30-oz.) box powdered chocolate drink mix
2 cups powdered sugar
1 (6-oz.) non-dairy creamer

Children can measure ingredients into a very large bowl and mix. This makes a large amount, which will provide plenty to give away. Store in an airtight container.

To make cocoa: Use 1/4 cup per mug, add hot water, and top with a marshmallow. For children, cool slightly before serving.

Variation for Mocha Mix: add 1½ cup of instant coffee to basic hot cocoa mix.

Yield: about 20 cups mix (80 mugs of cocoa)

Here are two other delicious drinks you may want to prepare for Father's Day or any day!

Banana Smoothie

2 bananas
2 cups milk

Children can peel bananas and measure milk. Whip bananas and milk in blender for a few seconds. Bananas will thicken mixture to milk shake consistency. Serve in cups.

Yield: 2 - 4 servings

Orange Blast

1 (6-oz.) can frozen orange juice
  concentrate
1 cup water
1 cup milk
1/2 cup sugar
1 teaspoon vanilla
10 ice cubes

Children can measure all ingredients into a blender container. Cover and blend about 30 seconds, until smooth.

Serve immediately.

Yield: 4 - 6 servings

SUMMER IDEAS

• Eat breakfast outside at a park.

• Discuss what tastes best in summer: hot soup or cold salad? hot cocoa or cold lemonade? hot chili or ice cream?

• Time how long it takes to unfreeze fruit juice in a paper cup. Take it outside to eat. Is it melting?

• Buy or pick summer flowers. Let children arrange them in a vase for a centerpiece.

• Before cooking pasta for spaghetti, show children how hard it is. Let them break a piece in half. After cooking, show children how soft it is. Let them pull a piece in two.

• For Independence Day, let your child help you plan a picnic. Our favorite picnic menu is grilled hamburgers, potato salad, coleslaw, watermelon, and lemonade.

Ten Ways to Keep Cool This Summer

One of the best things about summer is – it's O.K. to get wet. It's O.K. to spend time pursuing the comfort of just being cooler. Here are ten ways for you and your child to keep cooler in the house and outside, and have some fun.

1. ***Drink!*** Drink plenty of water, liquid, fruit juices, and hot soups. Be sure to provide opportunities for you and your child to enjoy a nice cool drink at home, in the park, or on a walk. There are lots of containers currently on the market for drinks. There are drinks with tops that pop, or squirt. Manufacturers make non-breakable cups with attached straws, or insulated sides. Take advantage of these important accessories not only for your child, but also for yourself.

2. ***Cook less.*** Serve more cold foods, such as salads, or do more on-the-stove cooking rather than baking, where the oven can heat up the whole room. You can barbecue; go outdoors to cook. Play with your child outdoors while the food is cooking. Cook bigger batches of items that freeze well or reheat well, such as rice, spaghetti sauce, or vegetable casserole.

3. ***Set up a "lemonade" stand.*** If your neighborhood is conducive to having a drink stand, children might enjoy playing at owning their own business. Modern lemonade stand owners might want to serve flavored waters, or juice, to cut down on sugary drinks. Help your child set up a table in the shade with a chair and sign noting what's for sale and how much. Limit the amount of time your child is out in the heat, and depending on age and responsibility, supervise the business transactions.

4. ***Have a "pretend" cooking session.*** Bring a pan or plastic bowl with cool water and spoon outside. Sit on the grass, a blanket, or at a picnic table. Encourage your child to stir with the spoon, or his hand, and add "ingredients" such as leaves or twigs. Serve it up on plastic plates. Pretend cooking and pretend eating are fun!

5. ***Enjoy outdoor " pouring" fun.*** Using non-breakable measuring cups, allow your child to pour water from one to the other. This can be done outside, or on a counter, or anywhere spills don't matter. Not only is this a fun activity, it helps with the fine motor control of learning how to pour.

6. ***"This is the Way We Wash Our Doll Clothes."*** Choose a few outfits from your doll or action figures, or use kitchen items, such as hot pads, dish towels, place mats, etc. Bring a tub of lukewarm, sudsy water outside. String a clothesline or rope between two trees or two posts. Help your child dip clothes in wash water and wring out. After washing, secure the clothes to the line using regular clothespins or doll-sized clothespins.

7. ***"Just Baby and Me."*** Take your child and their baby doll outside for a fresh air bath. Use a tub of warm water and real shampoo. Let your child shampoo the baby doll's hair. After rinsing with the hose, let your child comb and style the doll's hair.

8. ***Encourage artistic creations.*** For young children, let them paint the sidewalk using a pail of water and a wide paintbrush. For older children, first, use colored chalk to color the sidewalk. Then, let them use a paintbrush and water to lighten the colors in their creation, or to erase it! Be sure to look at their picture first. Take a photo.

9. ***Have a boat race.*** Help your child make a sail-boat using cork or tin foil for the bottom and a toothpick and paper for the sail. Fill a tub with water and stage a race. Whoever can blow the hardest will probably win!

10. ***Host a tea party.*** Take a tub of warm, soapy water outside. Help your child wash her child-sized, plastic tea set. Rinse and dry with a dishcloth. Then serve a cool drink and fresh fruit on your sparkling clean tea set. Invite a teddy bear.

However you spend your summer, have fun while you're trying to keep cool.

Sugar-Free Lemonade

3 cups water
2 tablespoons lemon juice
1/4 cup white grape juice

Children can measure and combine water and juices in a pitcher. Stir. Serve over ice. A refreshing alternative to sugary lemonade.

Yield: 6 (one-half cup) servings

Cranberry Fizzy

2 cups cranberry juice
1 cup orange juice
2 cups lemon-lime soda pop

Children can combine ingredients in a pitcher. Fill glasses with ice. Pour cranberry mixture to fill glass.

Yield: 10 (one-half cup) servings

Sparkling Apple Punch

2 cups apple juice
2 cups lemonade
2 cups ginger ale

Children can combine ingredients in a pitcher. Fill glasses with ice. Pour punch to fill glass.

Yield: 12 (one-half cup) servings

Active Young Athlete

Tanner is climbing the jungle gym. Mikeyla is swinging. Andrea is digging in the sand. On a field across from the park, Alec is playing soccer on a team with other children his age.

Children need to be active. Developing their gross motor skills is one of the important ways children grow. Organized sports for children are starting at an earlier age. Whether you are spending the afternoon at the park or watching a game, the activity and fresh air will help stimulate young appetites. You will want to plan for snacking.

What should you take? What is best to eat and drink while your child is being active? What if you are watching a game that runs right through the lunch hour?

"When children eat complex carbohydrates like whole grain bread and fruits, they can play longer. They don't run out of steam," says Laura Thomson, R.N. and mother of two young boys. She goes on to explain in simple terms that all food has to be broken down into "sugar" by our body.

White sugar is already a simple sugar - it doesn't have to be broken down anymore. If a child eats cookies and soda pop, it's going to be digested fast, and he will run out of energy. Mrs. Thomson urges, *"A child needs to eat what we all need to eat: healthy snacks made of whole grains, fresh fruits and vegetables."*

Avoid fatty snack foods such as potato chips and pre-wrapped cakes. Give choices to your child; let him or her help you decide what to buy.

Good choices for a lunch or snack include:
- sandwiches (1/4 to 1/2 is a snack serving)
- crackers, breadsticks, or rice cakes
- cereal mix
- sliced cheese
- fresh fruits
- fresh vegetables

When planning your grocery list include:
- fresh fruits and vegetables in season
- whole grain breads and cereals
- low fat, low sodium protein

Don't eat a heavy meal before any physical activity. Do offer a snack beforehand. Then if a game runs through a normal mealtime, your child won't get too hungry. Plan to eat after the game is over. Warming a pot of chicken noodle soup, such as the recipe on the next page, and having vegetables cleaned and ready in the refrigerator is a wonderful welcome home. If siblings are watching the game with you, bring something for them to munch on, too.

The following are suggestions for good choices:

Slice fruits such as apples, oranges, bananas, and grapes. (Treat apples and bananas by dipping in water mixed with lemon juice to prevent discoloring. Cut grapes in half.) Bring a blanket or quilt to sit on and a small cooler or insulated bag.

Prepare fresh vegetables such as carrot sticks, celery sticks, cauliflower, and broccoli with peanut butter or other dip. *(Note: to prevent choking, young children should not have peanut butter, and carrot sticks should be par-boiled and cooled before serving.)*

Bring water to drink. Generally, if a concession stand is available, it will serve sugary drinks, such as soda pop, and greasy foods such as nachos, hot dogs, and French fries. You will be glad you brought your own!

Guidelines for Athletes

No matter how young your athlete is, begin following these guidelines from the book, *Sports Nutrition* published by the Missouri Department of Health, for your son or daughter's best performance.

- Good nutrition is necessary for peak athletic performance.
- There are no special foods, food regimens or vitamin supplements that enhance athletic performance.
- Excess protein is changed to fat by the body for storage.
- The most important factor for increasing strength is not what you eat, but rather how you train.
- Water is the most critical nutrient for the athlete.

Eating healthy foods most of the time and especially the night before a game is important, too. Complex carbohydrates, such as bread, potatoes, rice, or pasta provide energy.

Speedy Microwave Meatballs and Spaghetti

This recipe for meatballs and spaghetti is a perfect meal the night before a game, and one of kids' favorites.

1 pound lean ground beef
2 tablespoons water
1/3 cup seasoned breadcrumbs
1 egg
1 (26-oz.) jar spaghetti sauce
1 (8-oz.) package spaghetti, cooked

Children can mix ground beef, water, breadcrumbs, and egg until combined. Shape into 1-inch meatballs and place around the perimeter of a 2-quart casserole in one or two rows. Cover. (Wash hands well.)

Microwave on high 5 to 6 minutes, or until the juices run clear (160 degrees F). Remove meatballs from casserole and drain all grease. Then return meatballs to casserole. Add a jar of spaghetti sauce. Cover. Heat 3 minutes.

Meanwhile, cook spaghetti according to package directions. Serve meatballs and sauce over hot spaghetti.

Yield: 4 servings

Amy's Easy Chicken Noodle Soup

4 quarts water
4 boneless chicken breasts
1 tablespoon chicken bouillon
1 carrot, diced fine
1 stalk celery, diced fine
1 (6-oz.) package fine egg noodles

Bring water to a boil in an 8-quart pot. Add chicken and bouillon, turn down heat, and simmer for 20 minutes. Remove chicken from pot.

Children can help add carrots and celery; simmer 15 minutes. Meanwhile, dice chicken. Add noodles and diced chicken. Simmer 5 minutes more.

Yield: 6 servings

Tuna-Macaroni Casserole

1 (7 oz.) package macaroni and
  cheese
1 (10 - 12 oz.) can cream of
  celery soup, undiluted
1 (3 oz.) can tuna, drained
1/2 cup milk
1 cup shredded cheddar cheese

Cook macaroni and cheese according to package direction. Children can help to carefully stir in soup, tuna, and milk.

Pour into greased baking dish. Sprinkle top with shredded cheddar cheese.

Bake in 350 degrees F oven for 20 minutes, or until cheese is melted.

Yield: 4 servings

Easy Sandwich Combinations

Grilled Cheese Sandwich

Butter one side of slice of bread. Place buttered side down in an electric fry pan or fry pan on stove. Place a slice of cheese on top of bread and top with another slice of bread, buttered side up. Grill on one side and then turn sandwich over to brown on other side.

Grilled Tomato-Cheese Sandwich

Place tomato slice between two pieces of cheese as you assemble sandwich. Grill same as above.

Tuna Salad Sandwich

To one can (3 oz.) well drained tuna, add onion, celery, pickles, and enough mayonnaise to moisten. Spread on toasted or untoasted bread.

Chicken Salad Sandwich

Chop or put chicken in food processor. To cut-up chicken add onion, celery, and enough mayonnaise to moisten. Spread on bagels or whole wheat bread.

A Rainbow of Recipes

When my daughter was young, she often drew rainbows. I think of this as a symbol of happiness. The colors, drawn close together in a semi-circle shape, remind me of the cycle of life.

Summertime is the perfect season to create a rainbow of colors to eat. The colors of the rainbow include red, orange, yellow, green, blue, indigo, and violet. The seasonal colors of fruits and vegetables lend themselves to such edible creations.

Here are some rainbow recipes to try.

Rainbow Salad

1 (3-oz.) package strawberry gelatin
1 (3-oz.) package lemon gelatin
1 (3-oz.) package blueberry gelatin
Water
Whipped cream <u>or</u> whipped topping, optional

Begin preparing this salad the day before you want to serve it. Empty the dry strawberry gelatin into a bowl. Add one cup boiling water. Children can stir the gelatin and water with a wooden spoon for 1 to 2 minutes or until the gelatin is dissolved. Stir in 1 cup cold water. Pour into an 9 x 9-inch square pan. Chill in refrigerator for a few hours, or until firm.

Repeat the mixing process with the lemon gelatin. Pour over the strawberry gelatin to create the second layer. Chill until firm. Repeat mixing and chilling process a third time with the blueberry gelatin. Again, chill until firm.

Cut into squares. Serve on a bed of lettuce. Add a dollop of whipped cream "clouds," if desired. While you are eating, ask your child to tell how to make Rainbow Salad.

Yield: 9 - 12 servings

Variation: Add diced fruit to one of the layers.

Rainbow Fruit Salad

Watermelon, cut into one-inch
  chunks
Peaches, pitted and sliced
Blueberries
Shredded coconut
Bottled poppy seed dressing

You will need a large platter to make your rainbow. Prepare fruit. Guide your child in placing fruit in rows of semi-circles to create a rainbow display. Begin with the watermelon. Make an arc of watermelon chunks around the edge of the platter.

Then place peach slices next to the watermelon, working toward the middle of the plate. Add the blueberries as the last rainbow color. Sprinkle the fruit with shredded coconut. Serve with poppy seed dressing in a small bowl in the space below the rainbow.

Variation for Rainbow Vegetable Salad: use cherry tomatoes, carrot sticks, and red or green cabbage wedges with blue cheese dressing.

Rainbow Muffins

1 egg
1 cup milk
1/4 cup oil
1 cup white flour
1 cup whole wheat flour
1/4 cup sugar
2 teaspoons baking powder
1 teaspoon salt
1 tablespoon colored sprinkles

Preheat oven to 400 degrees F. Children can put paper baking cups in muffin tin, or grease muffin tin. With rotary beater, they can beat egg. Add milk and oil.

In medium bowl, children can stir in flours, sugar, baking powder, salt, and sprinkles, just until all ingredients are moistened. Batter will be lumpy. Spoon batter into muffin cups. Bake for 20 to 25 minutes, until lightly browned. Remove from pan.

Yield: 12 muffins

Fourth of July

Families all across America gather on July fourth to celebrate freedom. Bands march and drums beat. It's a time for picnics and fireworks. For an Independence Day celebration, plan to serve a refreshing frozen treat. This will help you and your child cool down and supply extra water the body needs in hot weather.

Ruby Fruit Cups

Try this sugar-free, frozen treat.

**1 quart fresh strawberries <u>or</u>
   1 (16-oz) package individually
   frozen strawberries**
**1 fresh pineapple <u>or</u> 1 (20 oz.) can
   unsweetened, crushed pineapple**
2 bananas
1 lemon
**1 (6-oz.) can frozen, unsweetened
   orange juice concentrate**
1 cup cranapple juice
1 cup water

First, children can help prepare fruit. Rinse, stem and place strawberries in a large bowl. For frozen strawberries, do not thaw. If you are using fresh pineapple, adults need to slice off tough, outer skin and crown. Then cut the pineapple in half, lengthwise. Remove the core and discard. Dice pineapple into 1/2 inch cubes. For canned pineapple, add to the bowl; do not drain. Children can peel and slice the bananas. Add to the bowl.

Half the lemon. Stick a fork in one half of the lemon, and hold it over a separate, smaller bowl. Move the fork up and down while squeezing the lemon to release the juice or use a juice squeezer. Repeat this method with the other half of the lemon. Remove the seeds from the lemon juice, and add to the larger bowl of fruit.

Children can help add the orange juice concentrate, cranapple juice, and water to the fruit bowl. Ladle into 4-oz dessert cups or paper/plastic cups. Place on a cookie sheet and freeze overnight. Let thaw about 1/2 to 1 hour, depending on room temperature, before eating so the consistency will be like a slush.

Yield: 12 fruit cups

Frozen Peach Pie

1 quart low-fat, frozen peach yogurt
Graham cracker crust
Kiwi fruit, sliced

Let frozen yogurt thaw until soft, about 15 minutes. Children can help spoon into pie shell. Freeze until firm, about 2 hours. When serving, garnish each plate with a kiwi slice.

Yield: 1 pie, 8 servings

Homemade Ice Cream Sandwiches

1/2 gallon vanilla ice cream
1 pint strawberries, washed,
  stemmed and cut into fourths
15 double graham crackers
  (30 squares)

Soften the ice cream in a large bowl. Children can help blend in the fruit. Pour the ice cream mixture into a wax paper-lined 13 x 9 x 2-inch pan. Cover with wax paper, and freeze until hard.

 Turn the frozen ice cream out of the pan, onto a cutting board, and peel off the paper. Quickly cut the block into 15 squares. Children can place each ice cream square between 2 graham crackers.

Eat immediately, or wrap each one in foil and store in freezer.

Yield: 15 sandwiches

Ice Cream Social

Ice cream is one food we think of eating when the weather gets warm. And because of consumer awareness and demand, ice cream manufacturers have been creating a variety of ice cream treats that are lower in fat, sugar, and preservatives. Check the label to know just what you are buying. You and your family can discuss which best fits your needs.

Ice Cream Definitions

• Ice cream is made by combining cream, sugar, flavoring, and sometimes eggs. It is then frozen in an ice cream freezer, which stirs the mixture while it is freezing to prevent ice crystals. Ice cream is high in butterfat. Depending on the brand, ice cream can range from 8 to 18 grams/fat per 1/2 cup serving.

• Ice milk is made with milk instead of cream, which has about half the butterfat with 2 - 3 grams/fat per 1/2 cup serving, and sugar, and flavoring.

• Frozen yogurt is made with milk, yogurt cultures, sugar, and a jelling agent, having about 2 - 3 grams/fat per 1/2 cup serving.

• Sherbet is made with egg whites, fruit, sugar, and water or milk with 2 - 3 grams/fat per 1/2 cup serving.

• Sorbet or ices are made with fruit, sugar, and water with 0 grams/fat.

History

According to **The Horizon Cookbook - An Illustrated History of Eating and Drinking Through the Ages**, ice cream was introduced by Florentine cooks at an important wedding. *"Ice cream, the successor to water ices and sherbets, was born in sixteenth-century Tuscany and made its French debut at the wedding of Catherine de' Medici. It took 300 years before the French public, and then only the wealthy public, was able to feast regularly on this delicacy...by the middle of the nineteenth century there were dozens of (ice cream) shops catering to idle rich and aspiring middle class alike."*

During the 19th century, an ice cream dessert called a "bombe" was popular faire at banquets. A bombe is composed of layers of ice cream in a melon or circular mold or deep bowl with a candy or crushed cookie center. The bombe is unmolded, decorated with whipped cream and served with a chocolate sauce or fruit garnish. Other ice cream desserts are: Baked Alaska, in which ice cream is encased in meringue and baked; parfait is ice cream layered with fruit, nuts, and whipped cream; sundae is ice cream topped with fruit or chocolate (or other) syrup.

Let's Share

One way you and your child can enjoy the type of ice cream you choose is by sharing it with family or friends. If the weather is pleasant, plan on an outdoor activity. An Ice Cream Social can involve making ice cream or simply eating store-bought ice cream.

Ask each family attending to bring a topping, such as chopped fresh fruit, nuts, or syrups. Your child can help you pick out a topping and do some preparation. Summer fruits, such as strawberries or peaches, or tropical fruits, such as bananas or pineapple, taste great with ice cream.

For strawberries, rinse, hull and slice in half or fourths. For peaches, rinse, pit, and peel if desired. Cut into pieces. Peel and slice bananas just before serving. For fresh pineapple, cut off crown and stem end, peel (cutting out "eyes"), cut out core, and then cut into chunks.

Mix-ins

Flavor store-bought ice creams with any flavor of your choice. Below are possible mix-ins.

1 quart vanilla ice cream, softened, and mixed with:
- 3/4 cup peanut butter
- 1 cup cookie crumbs
- 1 cup blueberries
- 1 cup apple bits, sprinkled with lemon juice
  and 1/2 teaspoon cinnamon

Homemade Peach Ice Cream

2 cups (about 4) peaches, peeled
  and sliced
1 cup sugar
1 tablespoon lemon juice
1 quart heavy cream or
  2 cups heavy cream and
  2 cups milk

Children can help mash and thoroughly mix: peaches, sugar, and lemon juice. Let mixture stand 30 minutes. Stir in cream or milk and freeze in ice cream freezer (follow manufacturers directions), or pour into ice cube trays or pan. If freezing in trays or pan, stir every 30 minutes until frozen.

Yield: 2 quarts ice cream, about 12 servings

Crunch-Coated Ice Cream Balls

2 cups flake cereal
1/4 cup peanut butter
1 tablespoon sugar
1/4 teaspoon ground cinnamon
1 quart low-fat vanilla ice cream

Place cereal in a plastic bag. Use a rolling pin to crush. Children can measure and mix cereal, peanut butter, sugar, and cinnamon in a medium-sized bowl. Scoop ice cream balls, one at a time, into cereal mixture. Children can use a fork and spoon to turn, pat, and roll balls in cereal mixture. Place on wax paper-lined cookie sheet. Repeat until cereal mixture is used up. Freeze until ready to serve.

Yield: 8 ice cream balls

Lemon Ice

2 cups water
1 cup sugar
1 cup lemon juice
1 tablespoon grated lemon peel

Children can measure water and sugar into a small saucepan. Heat sugar mixture to boiling; reduce heat. Simmer uncovered 5 minutes. Remove from heat. Stir in lemon juice and peel. Cool.

Pour into a loaf pan 9 x 5 x 3-inches. Freeze 3 to 4 hours. Children can stir lemon ice every 30 minutes. Then cover until serving time.

Yield: 4 - 6 servings

Frosted Cones

2/3 cup sweetened condensed milk
2 tablespoons lemon juice
1 (8-oz.) strawberry or other
  flavor yogurt
1/2 cup whipped topping or
  whipped cream
6 sugar ice cream cones

In mixing bowl, add lemon to condensed milk. Add yogurt and stir until blended. Spoon mixture into ice cream cones to about 1/2 inch from top.

Stand cones in tall glasses or jars in freezer. Freeze about 2 hours. Top each cone with a tablespoon of whipped topping or whipped cream and swirl it around.

Yield: 6 cones

Sing-Along Ice Cream

3/4 cup milk
1 cup heavy whipping cream
1/3 cup sugar
1/2 teaspoon vanilla
Pasteurized egg product
  equivalent of 1 egg
1/2 cup chocolate syrup
Crushed ice
2 cups coarse salt

Children can measure and mix milk, cream, sugar, vanilla, egg product, and chocolate syrup in a clean 1-pound coffee can. Stir contents, cover, and seal with duct tape. Place this can in a 3-pound coffee can. Pack with crushed ice and 1 cup salt. Secure lid and tape with duct tape.

Children can roll coffee can while singing or doing another activity. The can gets very cold! Drain water, repack ice and salt every 10 minutes for 40 - 50 minutes, securing and taping lid each time.

Yield: 4 servings (1 pint)

Note: Do not use a raw egg because of the possibility of the bacteria salmonella

Frozen Pops

2 (8-oz.) containers vanilla yogurt
1 cup apple sauce
1/2 cup chopped nuts or
  1 cup granola
1/8 teaspoon cinnamon
4 paper cups
4 popsicle sticks

In mixing bowl, mix together vanilla yogurt, apple sauce, nuts or granola, and cinnamon. Spoon yogurt mixture into each of 4 paper cups.

Insert a popsicle stick in each cup. Freeze at least 2 hours.

Yield: 4 servings

Cooking is an important life skill. In addition to being a fun activity, children learn math and science concepts, nutrition, new vocabulary, and social skills, among many others. Working with food satisfies the natural desire to learn and to take care of our bodies.

Eating foods that are healthy gives us more energy. Good food helps us to be able to work and play to our potential through all the seasons—autumn, winter, spring, and summer.

About the Author

Cooking and writing are Amy Houts's two favorite activities. She enjoys cooking with her two daughters and has inspired young children in their love of learning and working with food while she taught preschool classes.

Her interest in cooking began at an early age. Because her mother worked, Amy was encouraged to cook and often made dinner for her family when she was in high school. After high school, her love of cooking and baking led her to attend the prestigious Culinary Institute of America in Hyde Park, New York.

Amy wrote a monthly column for twelve years, *Preschooler in the Kitchen*, for **Parent & preschooler Newsletter,** an international parenting resource. Her first cookbook entitled, **Learning Through Cooking Activities,** was written for preschool teachers and parents with young children. Her other books include **On the Farm, Winifred Witch and Her Very Own Cat, The New Jersey Quarter, An A*B*C Christmas,** and **The Princess and the Pea,** a retelling of the Hans Christian Andersen story. Many of her articles have been published in books and magazines.

She is a member of the Society of Children's Book Writers and Illustrators. She has served as president of the Missouri Writers' Guild on the state and local level and is active in her local writing chapter.

Amy has a B.S. degree in Library Science from Northwest Missouri State University, Maryville, Missouri, and has worked as a children's librarian. She lives with her husband and two daughters, Emily and Sarah, in Maryville, Missouri, where she works as a freelance writer.

Recipe Index

General Index

What Others Are Saying...

"A delightful blend of family fun, this cookbook will be a welcome addition in any homeschool family kitchen. Tucked away between its recipes are bits of history and culture, terrific field trip ideas, as well as fun family gift ideas that are sure to keep you cooking all year long."

—Nida Clayton
Homeschool Mother of 7

"There is a romance to food. It is not just to sustain us – it nourishes us in all our senses. Amy Houts imparts this philosophy in her book and it will be fun and instructional for children to go through the year exploring the seasons and holidays through her eyes and hands."

— Bernice Feldman, President,
Oxford Road Industries, Bakery Division

"This book can trigger some wonderful fun and meaningful traditions for holidays, events, and occasions. Simply written and easy to follow."

—Karma Metzgar, C.F.C.S.
Nutrition Educator and Mother of 2

*"**Cooking Around the Calendar** is a delightful combination of recipes, health hints, and seasonal fun for children and their families. The recipes are easy to make and contain ingredients that are simple and easy to find in most kitchens. Children will enjoy contributing their assistance to make these delicious foods!"*

—Julie Jackson Albee, Ph.D.
Professor of Children's Literature
Northwest Missouri State University